EDDIE'S OWN AQUARIUS

A Present to Eddie Linden,
founder and editor
of *Aquarius*,
on the occasion of
his seventieth birthday
from his friends, in recognition
of his contribution to English literature
and letters for the past forty years.

EDDIE'S OWN AQUARIUS

For Robert Hamilton:
Best wishes
Eddie Linden
Edinburgh
2014.

AH HOPE AHM NOT MISSIN ANY GOOD FUNERALS...

Compiled and edited by Constance Short and Tony Carroll

Published by Cahermee Publications

Book design and production
Tony O'Hanlon, Propeller, Galway

Printed by Impress Printing

Published December 2005

Cover and title page
Eddie in Paris, pen and ink drawing
Gerald Mangan

ISBN-10: 0-9551584-0-0
ISBN-13: 978-0-9551584-0-7

We are most grateful to the following individuals and organisations whose financial generosity made this publication possible.

Damian Smyth, Arts Development Officer, Literature and Language, The Arts Council of Northern Ireland.

Nick Mc Dowell, Head of Literature, Kate Griffin, Literature Officer and David Cross, Administrator, Literature, Arts Council England, London.

Dr. Gavin Wallace, Head of Literature, and Aly Barr, Literature Officer, The Arts Council of Scotland.

Whilst disappointed this time with The Literature Department of The Irish Arts Council, Eddie would like us to acknowledge the help that the late Lar Cassidy gave over the years.

We are delighted to receive the support of *Cultures of Ireland, that wonderful organisation chaired by Dr Terence Brown, Trinity College Dublin, with Director, Dorothea Melvin.

Madeline Boughton, The British Council, Ireland. Tommy Smith, `The Castle Lounge, Dublin, Marie Gary and Dundalk Town Council. Michael O'Brien, The O'Brien Press, Dublin. Maeve Binchy and Gordon Snell, Diana Hogarth, Phillipa Kidd and Colm McGinty, James Liddy, Emer O'Kelly, Antoinette Quinn, Frank and Oonagh Short and A.T. Tolly.

*Cultures of Ireland is an independent, voluntary association of individuals which seeks to stimulate awareness of the ways in which knowledge of the distinctive cultures in Ireland can encourage mutual understanding between the island's divided peoples.

Welcome to the **Celebration**

Poetry Ireland
On behalf of Poetry Ireland, we are delighted that Eddie has finally been honoured by his own issue of Aquarius, marking seven rich decades and a life's dedication to poetry, may he have many more.

The Poetry Society London
The Poetry Society Council would like to thank Eddie Linden for the efforts he has made over the years, his contribution to poetry and to the Poetry Society.

This book is dedicated to Mike Donaghy whose idea it was

Go nDéinigh Dia Trócaire ar a anam

Prologue

Constance Short

There is nothing more precious and worthwhile in the arts than the artist paying homage to her/his fellow artist. This special issue of Aquarius, the poetry magazine kept alive by Eddie Linden for over 35 years, is testament to that. Aquarius was successful because it was edited by a poet whose only aim was to promote the work of other poets, prose writers and visual artists.

Artist-administrators treat their fellow artists with the respect they deserve. We would not have over 100 poets, prose writers, visual artists and other friends honouring Eddie if he had treated them badly. He treated them well because he loved art, he loved the artist and he loved to be a part of this world. Poetry was and is his life's blood. There are many Eddies, well documented in the various contributions in this book but this is the essential Eddie and is the reason in the end why we love him and admire his achievement. Alan Jenkins in his response asked if this was to be Eddie's own Aquarius and I thought, what a great name, so *Eddie's Own Aquarius* was born.

When I offered to take on this project, I told Eddie that I would compile but not edit (to avoid being lynched!) and that I needed help. The first thing I did was to invite Sean Hutton to write an essay on Eddie and to translate some of his poems into Irish and thus I became an editor whether I wanted to or not. Soon after that, Eddie phoned me to say that Tony Carroll would be my fellow compiler/editor. Off I went across Ireland, to Galway, to meet Tony and this special issue was truly born. Tony was to become a fastidious keeper of the manuscript, gently writing to poets about their contribution when necessary, and compiling the history of Aquarius with Sean Hutton. I chased up the poets for the poems they promised, gathered the visual artwork and applied for the funding.

It only took two weekend editorial meetings and a few phone calls and emails for us to decide on the rest of the contents. Alwyn Gillespie suggested that Tony O'Hanlon be our designer. I decided the book would be black and white and we were off!

The plan was that Eddie would write the list; we would invite you to contribute. Every poem, visual artwork and reminiscence would be included because they were your present to Eddie. We would employ a great designer to make a beautiful book to reflect your talent and generosity and we would find the money to do it all and together we would say HAPPY BIRTHDAY EDDIE ON YOUR 70th BIRTHDAY and long life to you and Aquarius.

On behalf of Tony (who has chosen to write the epilogue) and myself, I wish to invite you the reader to join us in this celebration of the life and work of Edward Sean Glackin Quinn Watters Linden.

Love and solidarity

Seán Hutton

In praise of Eddie Linden

With all the classic apparel of the loser we have in Eddie a winner who is quietly getting on with the job. Jeff Nuttall (1979)

Elizabeth Smart, the author of *By Grand Central Station I Sat Down and Wept*, has written:

> Them I salute
> Because we can't go out on a limb
> Without guardians
> Like them.
> Eddie Linden for instance
> Let us hymn.

Poet Brian Patten has described Eddie Linden as 'one of the few antidotes to the poison spread by various English Literary Mafias', adding significantly: 'If Eddie did not exist, no one would have dared to invent him.'

All who know him, or who have read Sebastian Barker's *Who is Eddie Linden?*, will be aware of his Irish-Scots identity and of his Irish background, which has become more important to Eddie over time. 'Illegitimate', adopted and reared in Scotland, he left school at fourteen, barely literate, to take up a succession of low-paid jobs, becoming a member of the Communist Party of Great Britain along the way. When I first met him, at a meeting of Pax Christi in 1967, he had abandoned the Communist Party, rejoined the Catholic Church and become a pacifist. He was then a student at Plater College, Oxford, but he soon dropped out and returned to London. He threw immensely enjoyable parties in a Hampstead flat in the premises which he was caretaking and it was he who introduced me to a bohemian circle of English writers, gay London, and radical Catholicism.

Eddie reciting London 1994

John Minihan

It will be clear also from Sebastian Barker's narrative, as it was to those who knew its subject at this time, that his early years in London were extremely difficult for Eddie. As he sought to come to terms with the effects of the emotional deprivations of his childhood, his limited literacy and his love-hate relationship with the Catholic church and his own sexuality, it is not at all strange that he was sometimes a very angry and difficult person. He is recognisably the model for the Sammy Giffen, one of the chief bit-players in the opening section of Alan Sharp's novel *The Wind Shifts*.

It is true that the harshness of this portrait is partly dictated by the genre of hard realism, but the unflattering picture it paints is one of a character whose sense of self has been severely undermined.

In a poem for one of his radical heroes — 'Tribute to Archbishop Roberts', dating from the early 1970s — Eddie described himself as:

> ...play[ing] like all children
> With philosophy and ideas, trying
> To reconcile the Body of Christ with the earth.
>
> ... lost in a sea of confusion
> Now doubt[ing] the Rock of Peter.
> ...lost among the corn
> Yet wait[ing] for the day when a glare of light
> Might point the way
> Finding the sanctuary and tranquillity...

Yet the truth is that Eddie did not 'wait for the day'. Rather, he adopted an existential approach to mental and physical survival, seeking to locate himself through enthusiastic immersion in a plethora of causes and environments. These included the Young Communist League, CND, Catholic CND, the Partisan Café, the *Catholic Worker*, the 'Friday Group', bohemian literary London and the tenuous gay networks of the metropolis. By the later 1960s he had adopted the cause of poetry, as he had previously adopted the causes of socialism and nuclear disarmament, and was on the way to becoming the dapper, kindly, less troubled, still angular, unique individual he now is. In the process he has given his life interest and meaning, and gained personal satisfaction and a particular status from activities that had an altruistic dimension. In the process, he has also made himself remarkable and interesting to other people.

The occasion in the 1960s when Eddie, according to Sebastian Barker's account, 'pestered' John Heath-Stubbs to 'reluctant[ly]' give him his telephone number was a key moment in this progress, and one which led quickly to one of Eddie's most outstanding and durable achievements, the founding of the literary magazine *Aquarius*. This first issue, costing five shillings and with an attractive emblematic cover by Anna Mieke Lumsden, appeared in 1969. It was published from the address at which Eddie still lives in West London. Eddie S. Linden was listed as Editor and John Heath-Stubbs was the best known member of the team of Advisory Editors, who included Alan Smith, Gordon Heard, Cathy Tether and John Ezard. *Aquarius* 4 introduced the concept of the Guest Editor, who took charge of a particular issue.

In 1971 the first special, or dedicated, issue appeared. This was an Irish issue, guest-edited by Pearse Hutchinson. Issues 12 (1980) and 15/16 (1983/4) also contained Irish sections. Even when this was not the case, Eddie's increasingly close links with Ireland — especially from 1969 onwards — when he became a regular visitor to the house of artists John Behan and Constance Short in Dublin — meant that the work of Irish poets was included in general issues of *Aquarius*. The Irish issue was a prelude to other dedicated numbers: *Aquarius* 6 (1973) — a Scottish issue; *Aquarius* 8 (n.d.) — a Welsh issue; *Aquarius* 13/14 (1981/2) — a Canadian issue; *Aquarius* 15/16 (1983/4) — an Australian issue; and *Aquarius* 19/20 (1992) — an edition of women's writing. General issues and general sections, which facilitated submissions from emerging poets, were continued up to *Aquarius* (15/16).

Approximately one third of the issues of *Aquarius* — including the three most recently published — have had a different format: five of these have been devoted to honouring the achievements of poets and one to considering the poetry of the period — 'The Forties' — with which the names of the majority of these poets are associated. Issues 10 (1978) and 23/24 (1998) were to honour John Heath-Stubbs on his 60th and 80th birthdays. *Aquarius* 11 (1979) was to honour the achievements of Hugh MacDiarmid. *Aquarius* 17/18 (1993) was a special 'Poetry of the Forties' edition. *Aquarius* 21/22 (1993) was to honour the achievements of Roy Fuller, and *Aquarius* 25/26 (2002) to honour those of George Barker and W.S. Graham.

As *Aquarius* grew from the forty pages of issue 1 to stabilise at between one hundred and one hundred and fifty pages, and as the quality of design improved, costs of production increased. Eddie's determination that it would survive made him fertile in the location of the funding to support it. *Aquarius* had originally survived 'by a series of minor miracles', and on subscriptions and donations from well-wishers. Eddie himself hawked *Aquarius* wherever he went. From 1973 public funding began to be acknowledged, the Scottish Arts Council leading the way. The Welsh Arts Council, the Greater London Arts Board, the Arts Council of Northern Ireland, the Arts Council of England, the Irish Department of Foreign Affairs, the Irish Arts Council, the Canada Arts Council (Conseil des Arts du Canada), the Arts Council of Australia, the Arts Faculty Research and Publications Fund of Carleton University, Ottawa, Canada, have all contributed over the years. Special issues served as a device to access funding and the list of sponsors is a tribute to Eddie's persistence as a cultural entrepreneur. The prize for ingenuity in attracting funding goes to issue 15/16 (1983/84), 'a special Australian edition, plus new Irish poetry and general section', which was assisted by the Arts Council of Australia, the Northern Ireland Arts Council, the Greater London Arts Association, the Irish Arts Council and the Irish Department of Foreign Affairs.

In the less hospitable atmosphere of the eighties and nineties, however, even Eddie's ingenuity in finding new sources of funding was not enough to ensure the annual publication of the magazine. He dreamed of finding a millionaire; and Paul Hamlyn, the millionaire publisher, came up with £500 in 1991. Then Brian Wilson, Labour MP for Cunninghame North, asked a question in the House of Commons. An Arts Council grant of £2000 resulted. These donations enabled Eddie to publish the special issue on 'Contemporary Women's Writing', edited by the then Poetry Society chair Hilary Davies.

In 1979 Sebastian Barker's *Who is Eddie Linden?* was published. Described on the dust-jacket as a biography, this sympathetic account of Eddie's life was structured as a first-person narrative and described by the author as 'more of a documentary'. In 1980 *City of Razors*, a collection of Eddie's own poems was published, accompanied by extracts from *Who is Eddie Linden?* and an introduction by Sebastian Barker. More recently, in 2003, Eddie has received the well-deserved endorsement of the translation and publication of a number of his poems in the collection *Quarante et Un Poètes de la Grande-Bretagne*, edited by Patrick Williamson and published in Canada and France. This has led to welcome invitations to recite his poems — which Eddie does superbly — in France.

His services to poetry gave Eddie a number of public roles including membership of the Council of the London-based Poetry Society and its Executive. His achievements and his remarkable personality have won him the affection and regard of many. It was appropriate that Con Howard, Eddie's friend and supporter in the Irish diplomatic service, should have presented him with a copy of *Aquarius* — finely bound in green and gold — at his memorable 50th birthday party, held at the Poetry Society's London headquarters in 1985. On Eddie's 70th birthday we are reminded of many such convivial events hosted by his friends over many years.

In 1995 I attended *Who is Eddie Linden?* a play by William Tanner based on Sebastian Barker's book, at the Old Red Lion in London. I had the privilege of sitting beside the man himself, who appeared to be as drawn into the production and as mesmerised by Michael Deacon's representation of the character 'Eddie' as the rest of us; and as audience Eddie unselfconsciously and quietly reiterated the words of the script, which he appeared to know by heart. As the story revealed itself movingly before us — sifting the wheat from the chaff of personality — I realised why our friendship and affection had survived the ups and downs of the years.

Seán Hutton

Alice Maher

The Thicket mixed media on paper

Eddie Linden Poems

Translations Pearse Hutchinson, Anne Talvaz, Seán Hutton

City of Razors

for the City of Glasgow

Cobbled streets, littered with broken milk bottles,
reeking chimneys and dirty tenement buildings,
walls scrawled with FUCK THE POPE and
  blue-lettered
words GOD BLESS THE RANGERS.
Old woman at the corner, arms folded, babe in pram,
a drunk man's voice from the other pavement,
And out come the Catholics from evening
  confessional;

A woman roars from an upper window
'They're at it again, Maggie!
Five stitches in our Tommie's face, Lizzie!
Eddie's in the Royal wi' a sword in his stomach
and the razor's floating in the River Clyde.'

There is roaring in Hope Street,
They're killing in the Carlton,
There's an ambulance in Bridgeton,
And a laddie in the Royal.

Eddie Linden

Cathair na Rásúr,
(do chathair Ghlasachú)

Smidiríní na mbuidéal bainne
ina ngraiseamal ar na duirleoga,
deatach bréan na simléar, tionóntáin brocacha,
FUCK THE POPE ina scríobadach ar bhallaí 'gus
litreacha
gorma ag scréachaíl GOD BLESS THE RANGERS.
Seanbhean ag coirnéal is a sciatháin fillte ar a chéile,
        naíonán i bpram aici,
fear ar meisce glórach ón gcósán eile,
is amach leis na Caitlicigh as boscaí faoistine na h-oíche.

Bean ag béicíl as fuinneog thuas:
'Tá bruíon eatarthu arís, a Mhaggie!
Cúig greamanna i ngúis Tommy seo againne, Lizzie!
Tá Eddie sa Royal is claíomh ina bholg
is an rásúr ar snamh in abhainn na Cluaidh.'

Táid ag búiríl i Sráid an Dóchais,
is ag marú a chéile sa gCarlton.
Tá otharchárr i mBridgeton,
agus stócach sa Royal.

Translation by PEARSE HUTCHINSON

La Cité des Rasoirs
(pour la Ville de Glasgow)

Rues pavées, parsemées de bouteilles de lait cassées,
cheminées puantes et immeubles miteux,
murs recouverts de NIQUE LE PAPE et en lettres
bleues VIVE LES RANGERS.
Vieille femme au coin, bras croisés, enfant dans landau,
voix d'un ivrogne depuis le trottoir d'en face,
et puis voilà les catholiques qui sortent de la confesse du soir ;

Une femme braille depuis une fenêtre à l'étage
« Ça recommence, Maggie !
Tommy, y lui ont fait cinq points de suture au visage, Lizzie !
Eddie est à l'hosto avec une épée dans le ventre
Et le rasoir flotte dans la Clyde. »

Y'a des cris sur Hope Street,
Y'a des morts à Carlton,
Y'a une ambulance à Bridgeton,
Et un môme à l'hosto.

Translation by ANNE TALVAZ

Eddie Linden

Hampstead by Night

Comfortable little suburb north of London
With its wooded heath
Where queers and heteros nest at night
Little girls in mini-skirts
Boys with long hair and pockets full of French letters
Preparing for a night's fucking
Pubs flowing with artists
Conversing about their masterpieces
Not yet on canvas
Playwrights with introductions to the latest play
That they plan to write in their bedsitters
Writers with unfinished novels
Poets reciting their newest poems
That only find a hearing in the Rosslyn Arms
Or Leonie's parlour in Downshire Hill
Middle-class civil servants off-duty
Dressed in jeans for the weekend rest
Middle-class ladies hoping for parties and men with big pricks
Public schoolboys with effeminate looks
Hoping to win the hearts of butcher boys from Islington and Camden
While the comfortable bourgeois hide in their castles
On the top of the hill
And the rest of the bourgeoisie amuse themselves
In the village two stops from Camden Town.

Margaret Becker

Evening Light etching

Eddie Linden

Hampstead Istoíche

Fobhailtín seascair ar imeall thuaisceart Londan
gona fhásach chrannach
áit a neadaíonn hataí bána is heitrighnéasaigh araon istoíche
cailíní na mionsciortaí
buachaillí fadfholtacha ar bís chun leathair
a bpócaí lán coiscíní
na tithe óil ar maos le h-ealaíontóirí
ag trácht ar a ríphictiúir
nár dathadh fós ar chanbhás
drámadóirí le réamhránna na ndrámaí is deireanaí
atá beartaithe acu a scríobh ina gcuid suanlanna cónaithe
scríbhneoirí le h-úrscéalta gan críochnú
filí ag aithris na ndánta is nuaí dá gcuid
nach bhfaigheann éisteacht ach sa *Rosslyn Arms*
nó i bparlús *Leonie* in *Downshire Hill*
státseirbhísigh meánaicmeacha ar scor ón oifig
deinimghléasta don sos deireadh seachtaine
mná meánaicmeacha ar thóir na craice is lucht smíste boid
buachaillí aghaidhbhaineanda na gcoláistí mórluachacha
ag dúil le giollaí na mbúistéirí ó *Islington* is *Camden*
fad is a théann na buirgeoisigh rachmasacha i bhfolach ina ndúnárais
ar bharr cnoic
is a bhaineann an fuílleach acu sult as an saol
sa sráidbhaile dhá stad traenach ó thuaidh ó *Camden Town.*

Translation by Seán Hutton

John Behan *Eddie reading* brush drawing

Eddie Linden

For a Dublin Artist

He works in bronze creating matter in steel
Not like those who sit in judgment with jars of Guinness
I have seen them on high stools passing out unpublished work
While someone labours into the night amid the lightning flash of a welder's rod

His is not just of brain as of sweat
Nor do you find such a man in idle talk with fools in intellectual bars
Only in the gallery will you find the finished piece
And find the man.

Do ealaíontóir ó Bhaile Átha Cliath

Oibríonn sé le cré-umha is cruach ag nochtadh ábhair
ní den drong é a shuíonn i mbun breithiúnais ag diúgadh a bpiontaí Guinness
tá siadsan feicthe agam ina suí ar a stólta arda ag malartú saothair nár foilsíodh
is an té seo ag saothrú leis amach san oíche faoi stuanna bladhmacha bharra an táthaire

ní de thoradh intleachta amháin a dhéantús ná de thoradh allais
is ní bhfaightear a leithéid ag bleadracht le pleotaí i dtithe tábhairne na n-intleachtach
is sa dánlann amháin a aimseofá an t-earra críochnaithe
is nádúr an duine seo.

Translation by Seán Hutton

Dannie Abse
Helen Adam
Dermot Ahern
Craigie Aitchison
Christopher Arkell
Leland Bardwell
George Barker
onathan Barker
Sebastian Barker
Margaret Becker
ohn Behan
Nessa Behan
Oliver Bernard
Gordon Bowker
Alan Brownjohn
Richard Burns
Pat Byrne
ames Campbell
Tony Carroll
Mary Caulfield
Elizabeth Glackin Chapman
William Leo Coakley
Patrick Conyngham
Robert Creeley
Bernard Crick
Anthony Cronin
Hilary Davies
Gerald Dawe
ohn F Deane
Diarmuid Delargy
Fergus Delargy
Mike Donaghy
ulie Anne Duffy
Paul Durcan
Geoffrey Elborn
Elaine Feinstein
Katherine Gallagher
Patrick Galvin,
Sylvia Geraghty
Alwyn Gillespie
Alasdair Gray
Fiona Green
Martin Green
Gerry Harrison
Anne Haverty
Dermot Healy
Seamus Heaney
ohn Heath-Stubbs
oy Hendry
ohn Hogan
Con Howard
ohn Hughes
Pearse Hutchinson
Sean Hutton
Alan Jenkins
udith Kazantzis
ames Kelman
Brendan Kennelly
Bruce Kent
Ben Kiely
Marius Kociejowski
Ernest Lavery
Maurice Leitch
Tom Leonard
James Liddy
Michael Longley
John Lucas
Padraic MacCana
Enda McDonagh
Colin McGookin
Roger McGough
Brighid McLaughlin
Aongus Dubh MacNeacail
Alice Maher
Derek Mahon
Gerald Mangan
Gerda Mayer
John Minihan
John Montague
Mary Montague
John Moran
Andrew Motion
Blake Morrison
Paul Muldoon
Wesley Murphy
Patrick Newley
Eilean Ni Chuilleanain
Eamonn O'Doherty
Desmond O'Grady
Brian Patten
Glenn Patterson
Tom Paulin
Peter Porter
Robin Prising
Gabriel Rosenstock
Trevor Royle
Anthony Rudolf
Bernard Saint
Dermot Seymour
Clare Short
Constance Short
Elizabeth Smart
Tommy Smith
Damian Smyth
Sydney Bernard Smyth
Ralph Steadman
Matthew Sweeney
Anne Talvaz
Anthony Thwaite
Trevor Tolley
Shaun Traynor
Richard Tyrrell
Charlie Walsh
Joseph Woods
Macdara Woods

poetry
verse

Doodles for Eddie

The first hint of inspiration begins with perceptions not unlike
Those of a blind man picturing a performing orchestra.

By talking to yourself you can hear what you are thinking.

If you are happy do not ask too many questions.

Extreme pessimism is comic; extreme optimism, tragic.

The longer a politician remains in power the better he can say
what he means without meaning what he says.

Those two tall trees you saw leaning towards each other whose
furthest branches interlocked, the wind busy with their leaves,
were discussing the Pathetic Fallacy.

Only heretics are allowed to enter Heaven.

For your safety the doors to Hell have a fire-lit keyhole.

Every charismatic man has a woman imprisoned within him
trying to get out.

Envy holds a dagger.

We are never bored when we are in the company of an enemy.

Nessa Behan

Eddie at Christmastime 1994
original photograph
page 25

Dannie Abse

Gratitude is a temporary phenomenon.

Should you see a white butterfly, little solitary soul, staggering in a churchyard, rising above the stone tablets, then stumbling, then rising again like one learning to fly, have the grace to stand still for a moment.

To bury the hatchet is unfortunately a unilateral act.

Love your neighbour cautiously.

Lovers in bed are all guilty of word abuse.

When a tall person meets a small person, the latter stands up straight.

The strangeness of human laughter – as when the lion-tamer returned home and was bitten by his neighbour's Pekinese.

The sadomasochist is one who would do to others what he would do to himself.

Young people in the bathroom make faces in the mirror; old people don't need to.

Nothing depresses an author more than a visit to a bookshop.

IN
RI

Limbo Gate

They all were in the Limbo Gate
When Adam ended mortal fate,
The naked, the naked,
The hosts of whirling clay;
All the awful swarms of man
That trod on Earth since time began,
They were in the Limbo Gate
On Hallelujah Day.

Some were peaceful from their birth.
Some with blood had shrouded Earth.
They jostled in the Limbo Gate
Where splendid lightnings play.
'I was Jesus, Mary's son.'
'And I the lord Napoleon.'
'I loved.' 'I murdered. ' 'We are one.'
Green waves, and golden spray.

'I, a seraph royally fair.
I was the rabbit in the snare.
I, the fish that gasped for air,
The stag in jeopardy.
All poor beasts that felt his hate
And shared in Man's disastrous fate.
I am in the Limbo Gate,
Glad at last, and free.'

Loosened now from time and space,
The multitudes through Limbo race,
The naked, the naked,
On Hallelujah Day.
Immortal spirits dearly bought,
Or but the flickering of a thought,
A dream of Krishna's meaning nought?
Green waves, and golden spray.

Saul had slaves, ten thousand three.
St. Francis set the caged birds free.
Blake rejoiced in poverty.
Alexander rued his throne.
King David loved his harp to play.
Green waves, and golden spray.
Let gigantic Adam stay
Silent and alone.

Adam on his nuclear bed,
Venus blazing at his head.
Woman once, now star to shed
Light along his clay.
Adam sprawls in Limbo shade
By a blazing star betrayed.
Raging powers with which he played
Toss his world away.

Towers of atoms fall and rise
Where gigantic Adam lies.
Adam lies in Limbo Gate
Dwarfing night and day.
Eden's lark beside him sings.
No tomorrow lifts her wings.
Silence takes all living things.
Green waves, and golden spray.

Craigie Aitchison *untitled,* oil on canvas

Christopher Arkell

To Eddie Linden

Your voice, cursing the Pope
(But not your words); city
Saturday sharp, your lines as witty
As any of Connolly, poor Scotland's Hope:

You in the thick of it
Arguing an angry toss
With a first generation boss:
Yours is the clangour of a Lord of Lit.

I, an unequal friend,
(Out when you call) don't hear
Much of the loneliness, the fear,
Even the hope your raw-boned words intend,

Yet, Eddie, where you stand
(Now the banners are furled)
At that slight angle to the world,
Is where I'll catch true friendship, rightly scanned.

'Drum up a poem...'

Drum up a poem
They said, for Eddie's
Birthday
And me, as empty as
An upturned barrel!
Who then, is this
Aquarius fellow,
This Eddie Linden?
Is he some sort
Of astronaut
In the bend of the wind
That the poor folks
Like us remember?
Who did demons for us
As we struggled to climb
On to the empty page?
Good luck, so

To the beat
Of your Scottish
Irish heart
From this empty barrel
I send you
A drum of delight.

George Barker

To my Mother

Most near, most dear, most loved and most far,
Under the window where I often found her
Sitting as huge as Asia, seismic with laughter,
Gin and chicken helpless in her Irish hand,
Irresistible as Rabelais, but most tender for
The lame dogs and hurt birds that surround her,-
She is a procession no one can follow after
But be like a little dog following a brass band.

She will not glance up at the bomber, or condescend
To drop her gin and scuttle to the cellar,
But lean on the mahogany table like a mountain
Whom only faith can move, and so I send
O all my faith and all my love and tell her
That she will move from mourning into morning.

Sebastian Barker

For Eddie Linden On His 70th Birthday

The sprawl of language is the less
For what you are and I address,
Dear editor, my Eddie, who,
Shacked up in Sutherland Avenue,
Published four decades of verse
Uniquely in *Aquarius*.
No one knows how you became
The man behind the Christian name.
Or do we know? For what you are,
Like the formation of a star,
Comes into being like the sun
Closer now your work is done,
And we see what you always were,
An incandescent Irish seer
Toppling the icons of an age
On a microscopic wage,
Drunk as the sea where Skellig sails
All night the black Atlantic gales.
Seventy years, and now the face
Of granite obstacles in place,
Like love and death and bowel cancer
Erasing any easy answer.
So face the truth and face it well
My perfect friend in asphodel.

John Minihan Eddie with George Barker, 1991

Oliver Bernard

**Eddie Linden:
To Whom It May Concern**

Drinking in the French pub
What have I done to deserve
Being compelled to listen
To the concise autobiography
(And not for the first time either)
Of this wild eyed scrubby
Catholic communist working class
Glaswegian Irish peacenik?

Nevertheless years later
Having done nothing to deserve it
We are all being interceded for
Yes lifted up to the Lord
By His servant Eddie who claims
To be at best an unsatisfactory one
While an angelic whisper
Advises me to write him
A specially glowing reference.

Eddie Linden

His name…Eleven letters, with three Es —
Two I's — and two N's — one L — and three D's.

Try to get a good anagram from it
— You can't. 'LINE DENIED' — D doesn't fit

A poet. ID-NEED? — NIL, ED! A fair try…
E.E.LLINDEIDD…Well, that might supply

One Celtic element he wouldn't claim,
And give this Irish Scot a fair Welsh name.

The Reverend NEIL DILEE, D.D.? — No!
I hate this game, I'm lousy at it, so

I'll offer just this visual memory:
Of Eddie there on BBC TV

On *Question Time* one Thursday, making quite plain
His views on politics — then back again

Still raging on at a complacent clique
Of sly-tongued panellists the *following* week

And the week after, one of a crowd of faces
Putting the politicians through their paces

Weekly, for months, to give us the impression
That we were in for a rumbustious session…

Famous for fifteen minutes? That's not right!
Eddie was famous every Thursday night.

Note: In *Question Time* on BBC 1 television a panel of politicians and 'celebrities' answers questions from a studio audience. This poem recalls Eddie's impassioned contribution to one programme — subsequently included in a mosaic of audience shots regularly shown during the signature tune at the beginning. A.B.

Richard Burns

These Hands (from Manual)

1 These hands touch things that are not things at all
memories dreams absolutions victories reflections
these hands also repeatedly pick such things up
responsibilities disadvantages obligations loyalties
take them on take them up and refuse to let them go

Regardless of disputation dismissal attack and
despite ageing and the gnawings of doubt and pain
these hands are capable of latching and indeed clinging
on stubbornly to certain things that are not things at all
that nevertheless can seem more important than life

11 And this left hand of mine now packing this page with script
and this right hand steadying the same page's edge
together reach out to your hands that hold and turn
the same copy in another time entirely your own
or click or flick an icon to resurrect its appearance

which curiously means that exceedingly far
across time and space and despite our mortalities
you and I join hands through poetry in a kind
of peace and harmony that is unshakeable and this
is a bond and a pledge and a gift and a miracle

Poet of the Dispossessed
For Eddie Linden on his 70th birthday

The poet ploughs his own potato field
And plants his golden wonders in the soil
In Maida Vale, remembering Tyrone,
The market gardens of the Gorbles.

He cocks his ear to the blackbird sky
Under the awning of the Pizza Hut,
He sees the trousers of the dawn pulled on
Through the window of the Paddy flat.

A hunger gnaws the bare balls of his soul
To share his pain with his fellow man,
To pluck the apples from the highest tree,
To whack the juices of the moon.

Alone in his room he grasps the pangs
Of Ireland's pain and writes them down.
He networks poets dispossessed by fame,
Picks up the phone and wakes a sleepless town.

He gets things done by graft and wit,
His dogged bone drives home the truth that we
Are brothers only if we chose to be;
He breaks conventions, takes the short cut to

The favour of the House of Faber
Finds provender in huts and hedges,
Makes friends with bards hunched under arches
Of Waterloo and other bridges.

He walks with kings and talks with hacks,
Stalks London's streets as if he had no home;
A wren in flight of wild geese rising
Like a song above the grey wings' drone.

William Leo Coakley

For Eddie Seán Linden

Ballad of the Artists at Work

This is my friends' processional;
as you see, their cash is low —
look for them at their work by day
for all of them know their place, their place,
but the one who ships on the sea.

He was a carpenter, journeyman,
who worked at frame and form:
he opened the window to catch more air
but found Disorder crouching there
and went to ship on the sea.

One read plays to the mad boys
and brought them to the edge of the light:
the doctors in white drove her out
because her dress wasn't straight, straight,
to the arms of the boy from the sea.

One killed rabbits day by day,
grew sick and turned to men:
with his bloody wages he took pilgrimages
to Delphos and Bombay, Bombay,
like the one who ships on the sea.

And one is a Doctor of Philosophy
at Mrs. Wright's Academy:
his ladies love him for his proper air
and the colour of his public hair, hair,
he'll never ship on the sea.

One is a jeweller's sweeper,
she combs his dust for gold:
the roaches and scales she gathers in pails
to save for her witch's brew, brew,
for the boy who ships the sea.

The lean one fashions ladies' boots,
lives on an apple a day;
the fattest, that wicked man of god,
sings his parish awake, awake,
but never the boy from the sea.

And one is less religious
though she prays on her back and knees:
I'm sorry to say, she'll need pay
but give you at least as much, as much,
said the boy just back from the sea.

One is a lumberman's helper —
beware his hammering adze;
and one whispers, black power, black power,
all the White Way home, home,
to the boy who ships on the sea.

And one is a Poet of Renown
who lives on beauty alone, alone,
who lives by his beauty alone,
and none of us laughs in his pretty face
but the boy who ships the sea.

And I, alas, do even less
to earn my bread and meat:
I order zinc plates, and words and dates,
and work on the galleys, slave, slave,
and dream of ships on the sea.

Ask me in a year or two
if our ship come home;
ask me again in a century
but don't look under the stone, stone,
for the boy who shipped the sea.

Patrick Conyngham

For Eddie's seventieth birthday

Eddie Linden rises

Sometimes lurching though ever in defence

Of all that is poetic…..

Crowning moments of intense existence.

That honours and bestow enthusiasm

For living brought alive truly

From the cavernous comedy

Of this peculiar labyrinth,

With all its ill labelled blessings

Of joy and despair.

He frequently takes the contrary opinion

For the reasons of

Sparking further investigations

Into the real nature of sunlight.

Robert Creeley

Thanks

Here's to Eddie
Not unsteady
When drunk,
Just thoughtful.

Here's to his mind
Can remember
In the blur
His own forgotten line.

Or, too, lest
Forgot, him in the traffic
At Cambridge, outside,
Lurching, confident.

He told me later,
"I'm Catholic,
I'm queer,
I'm a poet."

God bless him,
God love him,
I say,
Praise him

Who saves you time,
Saves you money,
Takes on the burden
Of your confusions.

And my thanks again
For the cigarettes
He gave me
Someone else had left.

I won't escape
His conversation
But will listen as I've learned to,

And drink
And think again
With this dear man
Of the true, the good, the dead.

Freedom as Politics

Pick a big one if, as is common academic sagacity,
One attacks another to hide one's own inadequacy;
So, like Peachum to Lockitt, I abuse another
Who is my craft-master and elder brother,
No less than Professor Sir Isaiah Berlin
Picked not for any irredeemable sin
But for being, like a Liberal in love,
Reluctant to go far enough,
Sensing an impropriety in every call
On freedom made by rough political.
I pick no quarrel, just a bone over tea
With one of his *Two Concepts of Liberty.*
In his inaugural lecture, Sir Isaiah,
Oxford but modest, said that he'd require
Positive and negative liberty well kept apart;
If we must choose: the virgin, not the tart.
Positive is wanting some one thing so bad
That it drives German and Russian sages mad;
This view of things has come to such a pass
That zealot sees his leader in the looking glass,
And if I look in and still see reflected stubborn me
Then I must be freed from error, forced to be free.
Freedom as choosing rightly opens the college door
Is everybody else's nineteen eighty-four.
Negative at least preserves me as myself
Sitting down Don-like to a well-stocked shelf;
It means that I can choose between my coffee and my tea
But know that preferences cannot tested values be.
Now this is all quite so and very very well,
It saves me thinking heaven hell,
But gives me no idea how much to pay
As a fair price for liberty today.
Berlin walks so judicious, nicely and precise
That he trips up old lady-like on ice;
Liberty is surely not just taking care
But taking care at least to get somewhere.
Sartre and Hannah Arendt sensibly say
That freedom is living through the day
And living it in public view;
Is shaping, through some mutual pact,
Some hand-made thing which once we lacked.
Freedom is not avoidance of the State,
Like some unfortunate blind date,
Nor just an angry affirmation of 'my will',
It's more like doing something meant to fill
The social gap between the loneliness of I
and streets of demonstrators in full cry;

Bernard Crick

Something between lying naked in my bed
And dressing up to hit the others on the head.
Freedom is painting it, but not quite knowing what
Will follow from each original job-lot;
But it is painting it, not just thinking around
Projects which never quite get off the ground.
Freedom is how she always mistreats me,
But neither enduring masochistically
Nor is it just how I can kick her back,
But simply how we interact.
Berlin has little answer for the rude
Who call our freedom just 'a breakfast food' —
And so it is, but Dr. Bircher-Benner's Swiss Muesli
Which can sustain most needs of life quite nicely.
But don't measure politics by the aesthete,
I've no complaint at politicians cooking good red meat,
But let's protect ourselves from those who want it raw
And fed our heart's blood, clamour them for more.

Freedom was Cicero and Pericles,
Not T.D. Weldon on his knees
Picking hairs off Oxford fleas.

Freedom was Lincoln, Lilburne and William Tell,
Not Goethe's doubting gentleman from hell
With the Don-like negative soft sell.

The modern sceptic's version of the fall
Does not involve a tempter's stirring call
But simply not doing anything at all.

So ends my anti-Berlin for this day
In which — ungrateful wretch — I roundly say
That half-truths are just a kind of play.

Does cricket mean we always field?
And get the buttoned foil to wield?
Till left like Peer Gynt's onion peeled.

Life is real and life is free
To choose and make creatively,
Is wakeful coffee and not sleeping tea.

The Lives of the Poets

All the sad clichés of the old editions:
'An early disappointment of the heart',
'Habitually despairing cast of mind',
'His hopes of public favour dashed again',
'Long-hours of arduous and ill-paid toil',
'Constant recourse to alcohol and drugs',
'A constitution weakened by excess';
Spring up with wry renewable effect
As I hack out biographies tonight.
Romantic, minor, victims of their *zeitgeist*,
Cloaked in their common repertory despairs,
They coughed and caught their final colds and died.
'An early disappointment of the heart'.
We all might smile. But there is nothing comic
In Clarence Mangan's misery or mask.
And Dowson haunts the histories of fame.
Stab every cliché with an irony
Previous compilers did not know was needed
They're true enough of some, perhaps of most.
I between jigs and reels had colleagues also,
Mocked mockers, drunk with trouble, to whom now
I see such cliché dooms could well apply.
Does then the mere vocation in itself
Unfit some men for life? Or men unfitted
Turn to the childish refuge of the word?
Or is it that the practice of this art
Is guilt avoiding self-indulgence for
Those whom 'the public favour' may elude
And accident refuses to prop up
So that they stumble to an early grave
Under a compound burden: explanation
To make which is another crime?
Well turn the page again. An aged one,
Who held on past irrelevance and loss,
Smooths his grey hairs and leans upon a hand
Which opened lock and casket. He is fierce.
For all their lost authority is his.

The Pleasure Boats

A woman peers casually
through the angle-poise telescope
as day breaks on the yacht club
and the washed clean slipway.

A slow-moving tanker drifts by.
Already, they're taking full
advantage of the day -
pony-tailed mums keeping trim,

the recently retired who sold
the old place for a tidy sum,
and the staunch widows who marvel
at all the changes and at what hasn't changed.

I see the tops of masts, and above them,
the solid phalanx of guest houses,
with NO VACANCIES, facing the sea
that rushes in to the marina's red light,

where boy-racers will be parked tonight
under a fleeting metallic sky,
and the solitary dog-walkers,
and the girls, defiant, in one and twos,

and the pleasure boats returning,
and the rank of windows on fire.
So, tell me, what good was done,
what war was won?

John F Deane

For Eddie

Cambridge: a memory

Seagulls litter the grass in the city park, like a crowd
gathering for a rockfest; there's an arctic
wind blowing in on them though a hardy few
hovering almost kestrel-wise, test the buoyancy;
the sheened black of rooks startles amongst them,
their aggressive stomping, their perk. They feed
on something, yet all that sings across my mind
are words out of our shorn past, years we thought
God more violently cruel that we wanted to believe,
His 'just and chastening hand'; and still I cry
deep in the unsounding chasm of my soul, *out
of the depths*. My heart buoyant at times, at times
blistering like the suffering souls. The gulls
lift together suddenly, shifted by a yapping dog
and wheel away as one, crowding the sky with silence.

Note: At the Cambridge Poetry festival, many years ago, I drove Eddie Linden back to his digs after a reading; I had a blue Toyota Liteace van that I called, in those days, The Poetmobile. I parked it outside the city and slept in it. But Eddie had somewhere true to lay his head that night and I remember saying how poetry does not bring much financial reward along with it. We were crossing a small park together at the time; he stopped dead and caught me gently by the lapel and said, 'Out of the depths, John, out of the depths!' As I drove the blue van towards his digs we were stopped by the police; I was terrified, I had had a few glasses of wine, Eddie had had an odd glass, too. I rolled down the window, instantly pointed to Eddie beside me and said, 'This is Eddie Linden. I have to get him home.' That gentleman policeman took one look, seemed to know, and waved me on with a quiet, 'You need to get your light, left side, front, checked sir.' I nodded. Gratefully. Rolled up my window, and drove on. 'Out of the depths, John, out of the depths!'
J.F.D.

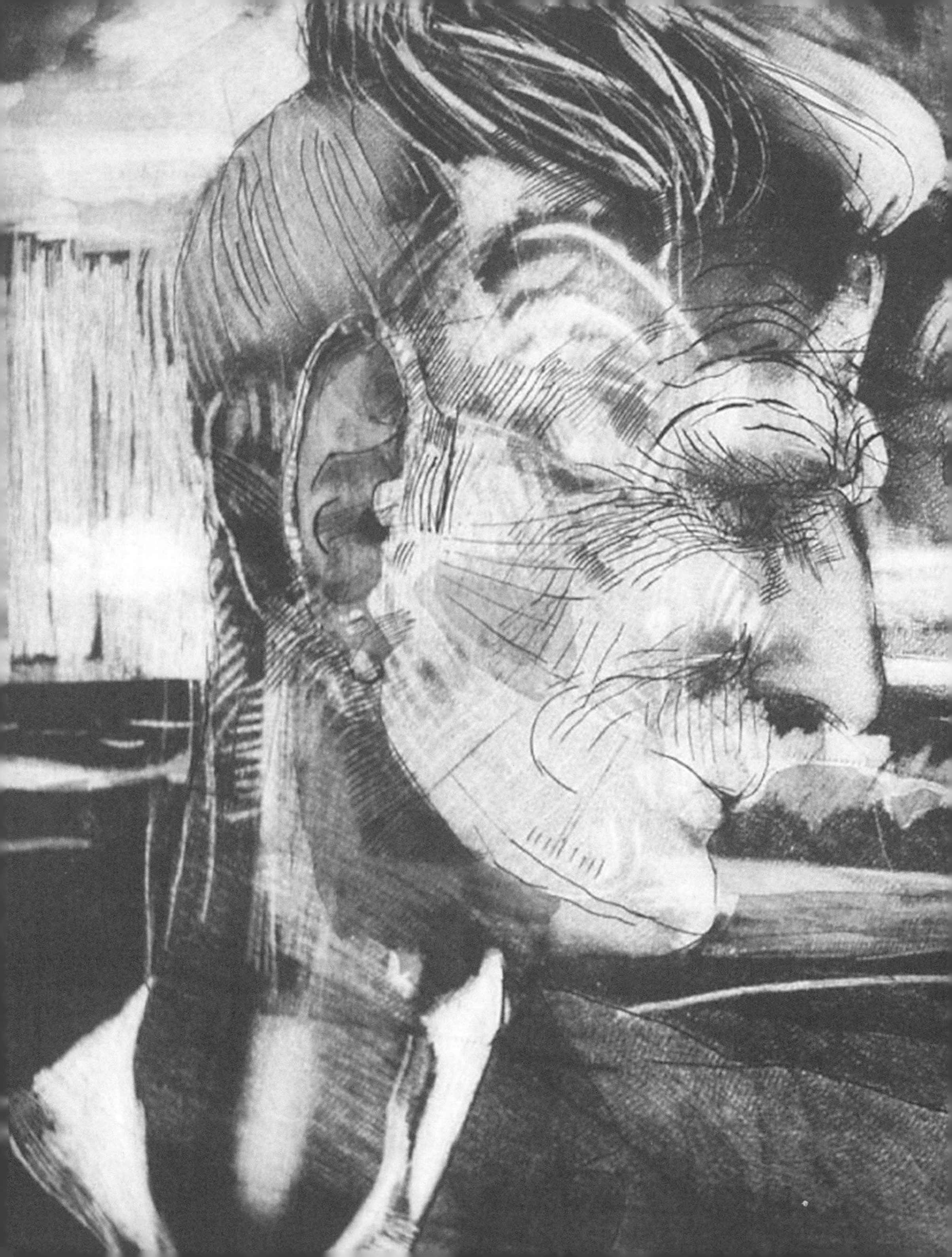

From Beckett Series

etching

Michael Donaghy

Quorum

In today's *Guardian*, the word *quorum*
Is spelled the same as *oqurum,*
The only surviving word of Khazar,
According to the *Great Soviet Encyclopaedia.*
Oqurum, meaning 'I have read'.

The original pronunciation is lost forever,
But I weigh three syllables in my palm
Against 'paprika' and 'samovar'
'cedarwood' and, for some reason,
'mistletoe'. I have read…

an entire literature,
and enacted all that it describes.
On a winter morning, in an ocre room
That we can never enter, the resonance
Of those imaginary consonants

The elders whisper over ancient documents
Flickers the blood bright shadow
From a glass of tea

Egypt

Egypt is packed full of fascinating history,
Powerful Pharaohs once ruled this vast majestic land,
In every corner is the essence of intriguing myths,
With it's wonderful scenery enhanced by golden sand,

And in the centre is the essential Nile,
It never falters always wide, straight and long,
The river is the life source of the country,
Its sparkling ripples sing their own gentle song,

Egypt is both historical and modern,
The land has a certain elegant grace,
It is an ideal country to visit,
All in all it is a marvellous place!

Julie Duffy age 14
great-niece of Eddie's cousin
Elizabeth Chapman

Paul Durcan

Carvery People

In the Carvery in a rainy
Country town a goose
And her gander wobble
Skew-ways over the plates
Of bacon, turnip and mash.
They do not speak, they gobble;
Creatures of the estate
In which we all are caretakers,
All geese in the goose-house,
Our beaks bobbing
In our fodder.
Astutely the duet
Squint up at me.
What do geese see
In a post-modern forager
With his beak in *The Sunday Times*?
Do geese eat *The Sunday Times*?
No, geese do not eat *The Sunday Times.*
Geese eat Dickens
Or Eddie S. Linden.

For Eddie Linden

Your wispy yellow hair and open face
have hardly changed since I first welcomed you
into my kitchen thirty years ago.

And no one I have met over those years
loved poets with more dogged purity.
Modestly, now, you have reached seventy

with those you honoured often fallen dead.
Peace and good favour garland
your pale head.

Ralph Steadman *Och!! Eddie* pen and ink drawing

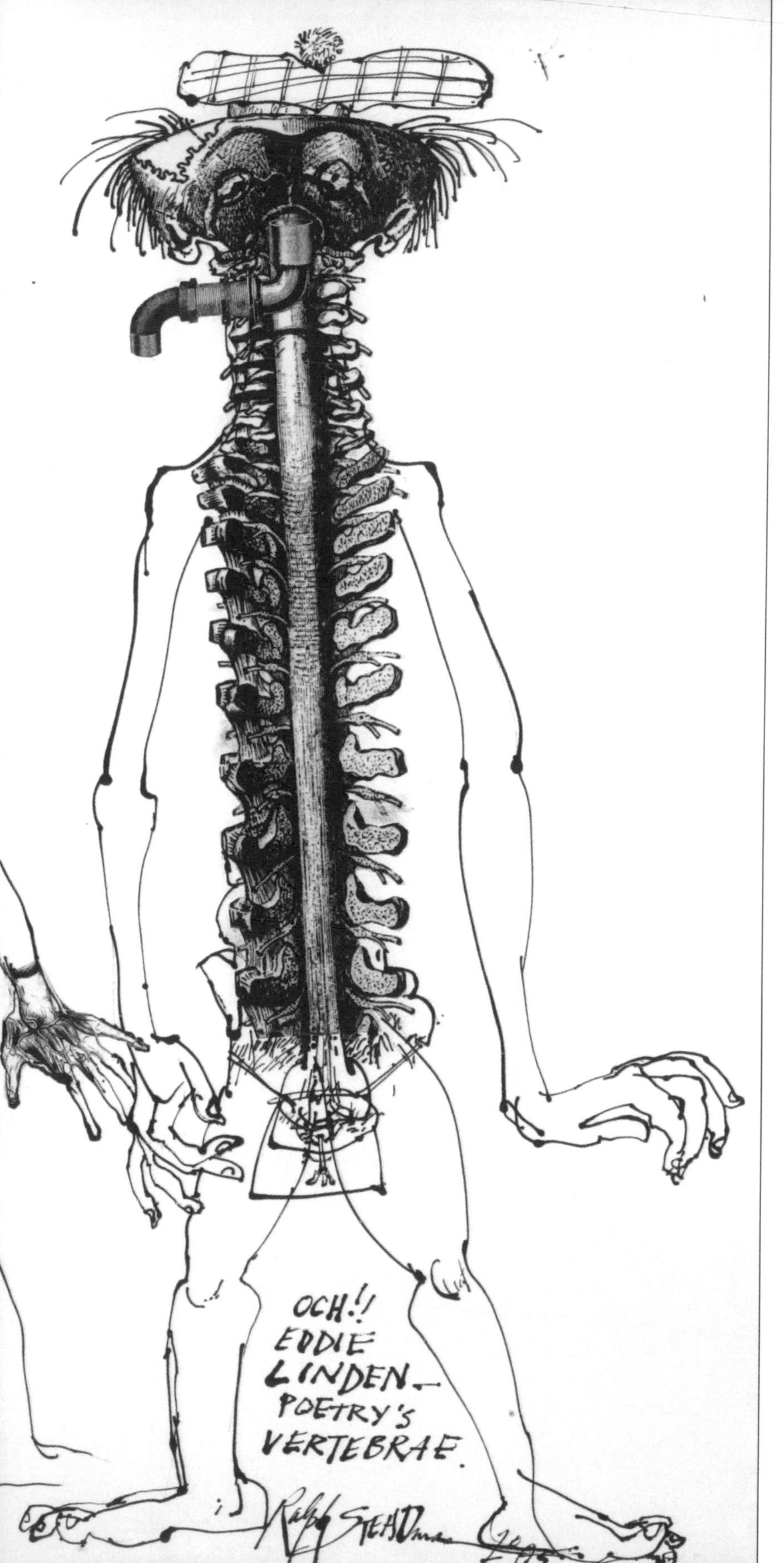
OCH!!
EDDIE
LINDEN
POETRY'S
VERTEBRAE.
Ralph STEADman

Katherine Gallagher

Hedge

Forsythia — my first hedge planted
with roots pillaged from a neighbouring tip.
I have watched it spread, reach out,
flag its statement — a yellow furore,
armfuls of velvet starflowers to throw
in the air, give to passers-by:
hedge-gold, this harvest I revel in
where yellow is traversed by sun
and the thicket locks me in birdsong.

I have been waiting for this golden rain —
for its sudden flux, lemon butter madness,
the flare of it showering over full stems.

I am in love with its brazenness; its ferocity
opens up the sun. This moment
is gold in the hand — mesmeric glints to shelter in -
a saffron-walled room en plein air, an alfresco walk
through found treasure.

Here is a riot, undeclared: tree-certainty, tree-silence —
each year a new layer as it spreads its yellow further, further...
No one writes this interface as well as it writes itself.

The Mad Woman of Cork

To-day
Is the feast day of Saint Anne
Pray for me
I am the madwoman of Cork.

Yesterday
In Castle Street
I saw two goblins at my feet
I saw a horse without a head
Carrying the dead
To the graveyard
Near Turner's Cross.

I am the madwoman of Cork
No one talks to me

When I walk in the rain
The children throw stones at me
Old men persecute me
And women close their doors.
When I die
Believe me
They'll set me on fire.

I am the madwoman of Cork
I have no sense.

Sometimes
With an eagle in my brain
I can see a train
Crashing at the station
If I told people that
They'd choke me.
Then where would I be?

I am the madwoman of Cork
The people hate me.

When Canon Murphy died
I wept on his grave
That was twenty-five years ago.
When I saw him just now
In Dunbar Street
He had clay in his teeth
He blest me.

I am the madwoman of Cork
The clergy pity me.

I see death
In the branches of a tree
Birth in the feathers of a bird.
To see a child with one eye
Or a woman buried in ice
Is the worst thing
And cannot be imagined.

I am the madwoman of Cork
My mind fills me.

I should like to be young
To dress up in silk
And have nine children.
I'd like to have red lips
But I'm eighty years old
I have nothing
But a small house with no windows.

I am the madwoman of Cork
Go away from me.

And if I die now
Don't touch me.
I want to sail in a long boat
From here to Roche's Point
And there I will anoint
The sea
With oil of alabaster.

I am the madwoman of Cork
And to-day
Is the feast day of Saint Anne.
Feed me.

(This poem appeared in
Aquarius 4, the Irish Issue, 1971)

Sylvia Geraghty

Ode to Eddie's friend, Miss Semicolon

She wishes she were a full stop
Or a comma like her brother
But she's just a semi-colon
Neither one thing nor the other

She's not an all-curvy comma
With tail wagging like a pup
Nor yet a more defined full stop
Who holds proceedings up

Today's writers try to place her
In the most unusual of spots
Then when Eddie reads the syntax
His face contorts in knots

In the Poetry Club some time ago
When it was getting late
She met a very sexy verb
But he just wouldn't conjugate

He said, 'There's nothing to you
You are nothing but a pause
You really are a waste of space
There's no limit to your flaws'

Since then it's all been downhill
Her self esteem now sadly stolen
She's retreated to the Irish Club
With her definite friend — the colon.

There, the colon and herself hang out
Clearly she is quite distressed
He drinks a pint — she takes a half
In case you hadn't guessed.

She drinks to forget the writing
Done by people who think they're smart
As she knows well, if they can't punctuate,
She'll capture no one's heart

So farewell you sloppy writers
She's tired of all the irritation
She's heading off to Maida Vale
To coalesce with colonic irrigation.

And Eddie dear don't feel bereft
She's admired you from afar
She'll call to see you later on
To drink a Birthday Jar.

Note: Eddie, your innate sense of good humour lulls me into offering this amateurish poetic rambling. I do so on your birthday, in deep appreciation of your scholarly friendship and advice during my time as Chairman of the Irish Club, Eaton Square. I hope you will recall that any poetic leaning I may have had, was nipped in the bud by the necessity to earn a living by 'sticking to the facts' (or at least that's my excuse).

This contribution is made in celebration of Eddie's lifelong careful approach to punctuation. S.G.

Birthday poem for Eddie

Let's praise the man who has two names
Eddie Linden, Glackin Quinn,
Born where they once fought King James
To let King Billy's flute band win.

Brought up in Scotland where they fight
(Celtic v. Rangers, one must yield,
Followed by fisticuffs at night!)
Is now fought on the football field.

He gave up God to follow Marx
(They share a birthday, did you know?)
When that light failed he walked the parks
CND banners led the show.

Then poetry became the cause
And *Aquarius* was hatched,
A magazine that won applause
And hope from failing gods was snatched.

Anne Haverty

Byron's Island

Byron went far
far out into the lagoon
in the winter of eighteen twenty-one.
Rising early he rowed all alone
a lone gondolier
to the little island of Saint Lazare
island of the Armenian monks
hoping to learn the Armenian tongue —
'something craggy to break upon' —
a break in the fog.

He failed. But who
can't fail in two damp moons to know
an alphabet he calls 'a waterloo'?
The alphabet teachers failed him too.
The teacher Fathers censored his work
told him about the Persian and the Turk
wreaking desolation where we were all begun.
They were fearful when he wrote it down
in his preface, feared
retaliation from satrap or pasha.

No more he goes
a'rowing. Goes back to the night
places around Saint Marks
the marks of his last waterloo
prefaced in his desolate look.

In far Armenia, he writes, paradise was placed
and there the dove came down as the flood abated
came to the Armenian island marooned like an ark
in a high church-purple fold of the Caucasus.

I too went far
farther than Byron
for in the autumn of two thousand and one
flying to paradise was easily done
and roving the streets
I saw like paintings unfolding
the faces of minor saints on Armenian people.

The Linden Tree

It's rare to meet a Protestant
Who says he's Roman Catholic,
You'd have to know your sean nós
And learn some psalms in Gallic;

Like him head out tow'rd *Aquarius*
For another dip in rhyme
And rear up fighting, fighting to comb
The beach for time.

You must have patience
To lead the blind poet home,
And go shopping in his dictionaries
For the word *ochón*, *ochón*;

Get yourself to the take-away
At night on Nottinghill;
Tot up the never-lasting
And let the temperance pay the bill,

Then turn up announced
At the back of the empty hall;
A few handshakes, go home unforgiven,
As if you had not come at all.

Oh let the catholic do the dishes,
The protestant sweep the stairs;
The Paddy's gone to forbidden launches,
While the Scot makes repairs.

The Linden tree is Glaswegian
With Northern Ireland roots;
You'll meet him on a side road
With a bag of wandering books;

And after the festival is over
He'll cross the street alone
Darting through all the dangerous metaphors
To find the underground to home;

A bible stop in Foxford,
A direct line to Dundalk,
An unsteady chair in the French House,
Then, Hampstead for a walk;

One day it's Listowel
The next Cheltenham:
Next a backroom in an unnamed street,
Praying not to come to harm;

Thrown off a train
In Perth, with his past left behind:
It all turns up in London, in lost luggage,
With the humour underlined:

In an old tweed jacket
That once was sycamore green;
For years he's nowhere, never heard of
And very rarely seen;

Rumours kill you quickly,
They leave you for dead,
I was thinking how'ta fuck is Eddie Linden
As he lays in his intensive bed,

And then he suddenly chanced
To ring an old number up at dawn:
'I've made it back to this life.
I'm ready to go on.'

Go on Mister Linden,
The key is under the mat;
Put your spirit in the kitchen,
Never mind, never mind

What happens after that.

Seamus Heaney

A Found Poem

'Like everybody else I bowed my head
during the consecration of the bread and wine,
I lifted my eyes to the raised host and raised chalice,
I believed (whatever it means) that a change occurred.

I went to the altar rails and received the mystery
on my tongue, returning to my place, shut my eyes fast, made
an act of thanksgiving, opened my eyes and felt
time starting up again.
                                        There was never a scene
when I had it out with myself or with another.
The loss of faith occurred off stage. Yet I cannot
disrespect words like "thanksgiving" or "host"
or even "communion wafer". They have an undying
pallor and draw, like well water far down.'

Note: It struck me that this poem (which I found in an unpublished interview) is as typical as it is autobiographical, and that there's probably some truth in it for most people who grew up Catholics in the middle of the twentieth century — people like Eddie and me. Alright, Eddie? S.H.

Eddie and the Weevil

Eddie Linden, biting into
One of my biscuits, discerned a beestie
Creeping out of a cranny — small and black,
With a trunk like a very miniature elephant;
Two angled and elbowed antennae
On either side of that snout, 'Who are you?'
'Who is Eddie Linden?' replied
The coleopteron, 'that is the problem.
I am Curculio, the biscuit weevil –
And particularly fond of Bath Olivers.
Mysterious providence, I sometimes think, designed them
Especially for me and my kind.
Eat me and I am additional protein.
In times gone by, the British sailor
Was all too grateful for that.
I do not question my identity.'

Joy Hendry

Eddie, Tigress Uninventable

Somewhere, up there, you're watching me.
You've been watching me for days,
weeks, months — all my life maybe —
maybe from before I was even born,
watching, waiting, to grip me.

'Jill,' you would say, clawing me …
'Joy,' I would respond, with Presbyterian reserve.
'Hello, Eddie.'
And, maybe, the tammy would come off.
(It took 20 years for you to learn my name!)

You've jungled your piercing eyes
out of the west-of-Scotland-Catholic-Protestant-morass
always yourself, declaring, declaiming:
"Ah'm a fuckin Catholic-Protestant Atheist-heterosexual-homosexual-bisexual …"
— contradictions jillfully multiply,
contradicting themselves joyfully.

The eyes have it, and we bow
to the naked energy,
the essentiality of your being.

Eddie always is lying in wait. Aquarian,
relentless champion, protectress, of those clear, clarion voices
the world would happily be deaf to:
Barker, Graham, Henderson, Leonard …

The Jungle is full of animals, but you're one
with a short-cut into the jungle
and out, way out, into the Milky Way
and other places we only Cream, Queen, or Radiohead about,
Mozart, Beethoven or Sibelius about
or Kathleen Ferrier or Callas about.

One minute you're in the gutter;
the next minute we're there,
looking up at those eyes.

Joy Hendry

Once saw you, myself, at a young and tender age
besetting a pacific Cambridge street
with a City of Razors.
Glasgow, not Cambridge.
But Cambridge looked down,
politely, not knowing what to say.

Taxis stopped picking up.
Silence fell. All stopped.
Eddie stridented West of Scotland yowls
into the daft afternoon —
its blue sky warm upon us.
Incomprehending shoppers disappeared
pursued by your eident banshee.

There was only Eddie, and the *City of Razors*.
And my heart leapt,
And the sky sang.

And then the eminent priest
(who shall remain nameless) —
you skulked behind my tall back
saying: 'Hide me from him. He's a fuckin poof!
And he's after me.'

I did as asked. No questions.

The claw still swipes our heads,
stalks us, hunts us down.

You've already claimed London to your tigress will.
You and Ivor Cutler, contradictory beasts
birthing out of a landscape nobody understands
but, in the wonderful way of the English,
they took you as their own,
as your own would never do.

You, Arnold Brown, Ivor Cutler, and so many
this still-to-be-Scotland is not big enough yet to accept —
what choice for you but tigress-ness,
what choice but to go — somewhere else.

Norman MacCaig (no less)
threw you down the stairs of Gladstone's Land
— the Saltire Society —
you had offended the propriety
of two Edinburgh ladies —
nae knickers a'neath the fur coats —
bourgeoisie an aa that.
Strange Prospero/poofter of London
keep Arieling the caller air,
After all, what would the Capital be
(10 million souls or so) without the odd tigress
up an unlikely tree,
snatching at the odd over-qualified literary jerk
passing by.

Prospero's wand got drouned
in mony pints o guid ale the nicht.
Ach weill. So what!

Eddie's wand, wet or dry, keeps us all 'Ready and steady',
thrilled to the mast
of the truth.
Not even Spike Milligan's teddy
could salve a night's rest if
Eddie's on the prowl.

Once the tigress has got you
in her maw, your best chance
is the happy admission of defeat
in the battle for all that matters —

And me, well, still
you claw me on …

Which is why, in the end,
leaves part, trees sigh
and the natives dance obediently below
as the tigress preens herself
in the highest branch she can find.

'Who *is* Eddie Linden?'
One-off of one-offs —
None can tell.
Honorary Aquarian.

Aquarian, unique spirit
in whose age we have dawned
you make *us* be what *we* are —
no quarter spared.

And you remain tigress supreme:
the unrepeatable, inevitable, unavoidable,
involuntary, inimitable, irrepressible,
uninventable

Eddie

John Hogan

Edgware Road Station

In the tube station at Edgware Road
a dancing figure, black and blind as night,
is crooning an incoherent tune
and repellent as a cut-throat razor,
his greasy cap maintains his space.

Through the mayhem of the crowd we breathe
a prayer to the memory of Theodore Roethke,
who spoke of 'unalterable pathos',
while the crooner reflects with mirrored glasses
a message in aerosol red lettering,
advising the world most urgently to 'FUCK OFF
and signed, 'with love from the youth of London'.

Beside us a frizzle haired girl consults
the dynamics of evil in the Sun newspaper
and the headline confronts us with moral outrage,
'SINEAD THE SHE DEVIL
Allies as evil as Saddam, says pop star.'

Note: The plurality of the pronoun is my way of acknowledging the influence my friends have brought to bear on my perspective. The poem was originally published in 1993 but it occurred to me that as little has been done to bring peace to the world apart from London Transport's courageous stance on busking, perhaps the poem still has some timely relevance. There are many issues still to be confronted such as the effrontery of pop stars, aviator glasses etc. And my poem is my testament. Happy birthday Eddie! J.H.

John Hughes

The Brains of the Operation

In the course of hunting feral cats and wounded foxes,
Driving tanker-loads of diesel and van-loads of *Embassy Regal,*
I cross the border a hundred times a day.

At Lifford, I rest beneath the oaks till noon,
At Killea, I pull rushes from under the feet of old men,
On Clady bridge I swallow the pebbles that line my pockets.

Ever since I witnessed my barber being shot in the head
By a retard whose hair he'd cut since the age of seven,
I have believed 32 is a magical number.

I can wake in a ditch with a thousand pounds in my pocket
And know nothing of how they came to be there.
I'm a rare creature for I can smell blood from a mile off.

Often I'm dragged into the back of a Land Rover or a Ford Granada
To have my privates twisted and pulled
By slack-jawed peelers who think it is a kind of party game.

For a week now I've made camp on the shores of Mullaghmore,
Where I make note of stars that have not been seen
Since the night before Lord Mountbatten went the way of all flesh.

I'm a man who can swallow his own hand,
Who has never told a joke against himself,
Who knows the etymology of *saveloy.*

Alan Jenkins

to Eddie

from The Sailor's Memory

Conspirators' pubs
In Deptford, pints,
Longley and Heath-Stubbs
Holding forth
On Hecuba, Drue Heinz
And Heaney's *North*;

Old salts
Who knew the ropes!
I'd navigated
This far, waited
In Davy's Vaults
With my fears and hopes

And taken orders
From half the crew —
Morrison, Raine,
Mahon and you —
Repelled all boarders
And stayed half-sane

But going under
By closing time
I heard with wonder
A known bell chime
From a life-raft
As someone laughed:

Willows, horse-chestnuts
Shade the water-butts
Of your childhood,
In river-shallows
Sunlight and swallows
Flickered, and driftwood

Noses to the sea;
The dawning of the age
Of power and poetry
Will show you a course,
Eyes on the page,
Reading yourself hoarse!

They'd thrown a line
To one who, drowning,
Was hauled back
From the brink, the brine,
To this new tack;
Your whole face frowning,

You said the next watch
Was mine, and poured
A grog ration
(Though it was scotch)
To stoke my passion –
Son, welcome aboard!

Fergus Delargy

coolvision

Odysseus Speaking

Deported, hunted out to sea.
many strange creatures. Many, many.

Fleeing, then everything down to the fishes.
Many trailing in the ship's wash,

fended off as they drown, by the oars
of huge machineries. Thrown on bars

when we try landing. We are
eaten for breakfast, lunch and dinner.

Who knows what we dream or hope for:
cuckoo-cry or cloud landfall,

just as the white flank of the halcyon
scoots by the unknown supposed island.

Build up of vapour mountains,
or a mainland as high as heaven?

Some of us go to heaven.
And some swallow the sea down

to our big bellies, don't sink but swim,
never worry there's nothing over the rim,

fear nothing and no one.
They're as simple as lions and I am one.

Note: I've included this poem about the old heroic wanderer because we're all wanderers and the last two lines are especially for Eddie. J.K.

What the sea brings

There was a girl once, she wrote a poem,
the sea brought it in.

The priest said it was a sin.
Sergeant Kelly
read it to my mother.
'Look,' he said, 'at what the sea brings.'

It brings foamsecrets
and trinkets and letters from the dead,
boys and girls in my father's head.

It brings first editions of songs
and lays them at my feet
like whispered words of encouragement
one cold morning going to school.

It brings the image of my daughter
twinkling in my mind
running up steps to me
electric with mischief.

She thinks the sea is a mod, not a punk.

What the sea brings is the sea's business.
The cliffs are important, the rocks lumpy and wet.

I give what I can.
I take what I get.

Pawnshop Window in Belfast

Minimised among the miscellaneous
faded artefacts and bric-á-brac
enshrined in dust-collecting velvet.
Two metal crosses, each inscribed 'For Valor'
The highest tribute a nation can bestow.

Commensurate with two men's sweet
tomorrows
and their invested yesterdays.
Casualties from Falls and Shankill
Expended in a different kind of war.
Their bravery's up for sale at 'Uncle Joe's'.

Communities; perpetually divided
where agitators urge sporadic strife
avenging ancient wrongs with bomb and bullet.
Where misdirected culture and religion
Engenders hatred strong enough to kill

Policemen, British soldiers and civilians
No value placed upon their families' loss
Like these awarded useless hunks of metal
Sold to 'Uncle Joe' by grieving widows
To try and feed the kids and pay the bills...

Colin Mc Gookin

Portrait of Eddie

oil on canvas

Tom Leonard

The Aquarian

The base the same:
the place
set out from, returned to
always there.

Not the place of origin
worn on the sleeve and/or
in the larynx;
nor the childhood saddled with.

Nor metropolitan litterati
tholed,
benignly patronising
'incorrigible provincial character'
'rough diamond' shit;
bolstering
imagined counterpoint.

That can pass
a handy hour
in decoy.

It gets boring but.

In reality it's consistency
of application;
focus of belief,
concern outside the self
held, over a lifetime.

yirraw right, Eddie
–yill day

you're all right, Eddie
you'll do
here's tay yi
here's to you

Londoner

on 3 score & 10

James Liddy

Who is my neighbour, Eddie Linden is my neighbour

Eternity
'What's the first thing you'd like here?'
'I'll take a No. 2 and No. 3 Pimms Cup, Mr Wilde.'

Love and Jealousy
I won't put up with it I will put up with it

What Finn said
The music of the pants that passes

Omós do Brendan Behan
He was a married man
He came at me like a bull
I adored the tresses of his hair

Pro Defunctis
Let us invoke the dead
For five minutes of memory
In pyjamas underpants when they took them off.

For Eddie Linden at Seventy

I'm thinking of the Pope and you, Eddie,
As I dander towards the New York Public
Library to peek at the field note-books
Of Edward Thomas wandering in England
In pursuit of spring before poetry and war.
Somewhere between Dorval and La Guardia
I encountered John Paul among the clouds
Like a surge of energy from the engines.
Now he lies stiff and full of chemicals
In precarious white hat and purple slippers
Saying the rosary over and over.
It all depends on the embalmer's craft.
The Poles cry out for his leathery heart.
John Paul was *musarum sacerdos* (part-time)
And you, Eddie, are a priest of the muses too
(Aquarian Order), your Vatican City
All the practitioners, the bad and good.
A shell blast killed Edward, a gust of air
That still riffles the pages in the library
On this bright popeless early April day.
Through the Door of the Sacraments I follow
John Paul and Edward and Eddie Linden.

Dermot Seymour

Ming Ming was dumped
on the road to Glaslough
by South Tyrone Batallion
of P.A.F. 1996

oil on canvas

John Lucas

ANACREONTIC

"*Boro na prospatho ena poto*"
"May I offer you a drink?" My first Greek words,
and taught me by a mischievous friend that other Edward
(Thomas) would have approved, his eye dark
as any sea urchin glimpsed through Saronic blue,

or, as here, through smoke lapping the tavli-boards
and that round, zinc-topped table where we crouched over ouzo,
its milky aniseed tang set off by globed
olives, frustrums of cheese, and sardine slivers
salt as each laugh and oath: "*Bravo!*" "*Malakas!*"

From ouzerie to packed taverna, then, and hours later
a final jug of retsina is put before us. "To brush
your teeth" . Babi the propietor's largesse
and goodnight blessing that means "see you tomorrow"
"*Tha sas vlepo avrio.*" So here's to you, Eddie,

and many tomorrows yet to brush your teeth.

Padraic MacCana

An Ode for Madge Herron 1915 – 2002

for her friend Eddie S. Linden on his 70th birthday

To visit her grave don't take
The road from Letterkenny
Across lovely Meenaroy
Its memories of red headed fighters
Take instead the road
That runs west of Ballybofey
That sources the river Finn
Past O'Donnell's castle
And the house of the kings of fiddling
Who opened the gates for steam.

Men under sentence of death
Fled here and were given protection
Among whins and thatching and whitewash
As did the clans on retreat
Who built on the watery leitirs
After fighting at Scarıffholaıs
The last Cromwellian defeat.

One hill named Croc na n-Each
Called after the riderless horses
Srath na Bratoıge so called
For the blood they hung on the branches
As the river dyed to their washed wounds
And somewhere there is a spot
Called in the Gaelic for grieving.

It was here that she found her repose
After her rumpus of living
The Lord will have sport with Madge
Said the priest who lowered her ashes
To accompany Sally Mac Geehan's
Whose ancestors came from the Blaskets.

It was the same old story
The cobbler's children unshod
Her father fond of the bottle
A tailor sewing for others
One coat between two daughters
Attended both Sunday masses
The coat changing hands in a limekiln
Them thinking that nobody noticed.

A masterclass she taught me
Among her cats and whippets
In her room on Fortess Road
Dropping three spoons on the floor
And athletically gleaning them up
That's grace she said for a poet
No college will teach you that
Me forgiven for thinking
Death could not dent or damage
This fortress of body and voice
Who lived on the brink of the precipice.

When men were dying of hunger
This bone house unentered by man
This mistress of scrubbing brush wept
Recalling her own starvation.
She who sat at the psychic crevasse
Fishing up a beautiful angst
Barnfuls of childhood pain
Fresh as berries and water.

Inheritor of the Homeric
This tempest on two feet
An uncontainable torrent
Defender of the absent friend
Critic of the corrupt
Friend of the disadvantaged
A swallow skimming the grazing
A full moon turned her hyper
Architect of the tantrum
A smoking volcano on shoes
A coin thrown to a busker
Resident of the dangerous bearna

Padraic MacCana

She was a tune on a fiddle
She was a tonic on Monday
Lover of whippets and horses
Poet of bulls and rutting
A goat for luck with the cattle
Critic of rifles and helmets
She was the cuckoo in April
A corncrake endangered by scything
Alternative voice of the times
Fearless critic of the phoney
Detester of toady and tout
Beauty never asked to the Ball
A flower far up the mountain
Blue bells for a May altar.
God keep her safe in your pocket.

I hope she likes this better
Than the last poem I wrote
When I had her hitching north
Of London town to her roots
Among churns and sheep and churches
To the glen of the nine brothers
A landscape too lovely for language
Screig all rocky above her
An Empire of terrible truth
Who had no need of a clinic
To dub her schizoid and loony
Solas na bhflaıtheas uırthı.

Note:
The kings of fiddling, a famous fiddling family, the Simis, (Dogherty) for whom there is a memorial in Fintown graveyard.
Bearna, a reference to bearna baoıl, the gap of danger (Gaelic)
Leıtır, a wet hillside. (Gaelic)
Solas na bhflaıtheas uırthı, May she enjoy the happiness of Heaven. (Gaelic)

Madge's birthplace, Glen na mbuachaıll, got its name allegedly from one local family of nine boys. No college will teach you that. Madge knew that I had just completed four years of university study.

Madge's first language was Donegal Gaelic of the Fintown Parish. She once told me that writers and poets would visit the psychiatrist R.D.Laing hoping to be confirmed schizophrenic.

Eddie Linden's mother, a Glackin, was also Donegal born or has family links with that county.
P. MacC

Eddie, I wanted
to compose a virelai
of seventy lines

But I don't have time
Not even for a sonnet
Will a haiku do?

Or three? Just fifteen
syllables left to wish you
A Happy Birthday!

Aongus Dubh Mac Neacail

an uairsin

de eideard linden @ 70

theirte gu bheil lusan ann
nach fosgail blàth ach
uair san linne, theirte gu bheil
lusan ann nach dùisg ach nuair
a tha an dearbh bhoinne braoin
a' bualadh orra a tha dhìth
airson a mhosglaidh ged
a bheireadh e gu sìorraidh
  gabh tlachd as am foighidinn
tha bàird ann dha'm b'fheàrr
a bhi dìamhair, a' rùsal
chalaidean an smuaintean
ann an còsan sgàileach
mar éisg tha tàmh an grunnd
na mara gun fhor na iarraidh
air an t-soillse nach toireadh
ach ainm is doille dhaibh
  gabh tlachd as an saimhrigheachd
b'fheàrr leamsa bhi leis na coin a tha
beò ameasg treallaich an t-saoghail
togail leugan na diachuimhn beairtich
is a' cuimhneachadh air an iomadh uair
a chaidh sinn a dh'iasgach nan sràid,
an uairsin, airson cuirm agus còmhradh -
mar a mhair ar trusadh na shuaichneas,
cluaran òrach nach seac 's nach searg
  gabh tlachd as a chrùn smiorail ud

then

for eddie linden @ 70

there are said to be plants
that only release blooms
once per century, it's said there are
plants that only waken
when the very drop of moisture
touches them that's needed
for that stirring though
it might take forever
  take pleasure from their patience
there are poets who prefer
to stay secret, scraping
the harbours of their thoughts,
in shadowed recesses
like fish inhabiting the sea's
floor neither heeding nor wanting
the light that would only
name and blind them
  take pleasure from their contentment
i prefer to be among the dogs that
live among the world's detritus
picking gems from rich forgetfulness
and remembering the many times
we went trawling the streets,
then, for parties for conversations -
how our harvest survives as an emblem,
a golden thistle that won't wither or fade
  take pleasure from that hardy crown

Gerald Mangan

Eddie in Edinburgh
pen and ink drawing

Eddie in Edinburgh #2 : A stroll on Arthur's Seat with Aonghas MacNeacail

Derek Mahon

from **Cyrano de Bergerac**
after Rostand

What, fame and fortune? But there's nothing worse!
I pick a powerful sponsor, lick his arse
and rise by stealth instead of my own force
like ivy crawling up a rotten branch?
No, thank you. Raise funds like the usual bunch
by spouting received wisdom? Act the clown
to please some fashionable art tycoon
who pays the piper, therefore calls the tune?
Ingratiate myself with the academy,
do daily push-ups for the bourgeoisie?
No, thank you. Make a point of imitation,
suiting my style to the most recent fashion,
ironically of course? No thank you; better
an unknown rarity than a crowd-pleasing writer.
Grace nouveau houses with my honest poetry,
the cynosure of a slick coterie?
Suck up to editors and opinion makers
to win prizes devised by corrupt jokers?
Discover genius only in the trite
and live in fear of journalist spite?
Be wretched if my innovative lines
go unremarked in the best magazines?
No, cheap ambition's never been my thing,
celebrity, influence; but to dream, to sing,
to laugh, write as I please and act from choice
with a clear eye and my own distinctive voice;
at the very least to strike out with panache,
amaze a gaping audience, cut a dash
and fight for my convictions, not for cash
and fame, but for uncontaminated air;

to fly alone, even to the moon up there.
Do you not see the virtue in being rude?
I'm sick and tired of the prescribed attitude.
I write nothing that doesn't come from the heart
so I can say, sincerely on my part,
I'm satisfied with the modest flowers I find,
knowing they've grown in my own patch of ground;
then, if at last I win some recognition,
it's not the result of a base calculation
since I take pride in the thing for its own sake.
I'm not the ivy clinging to the bark
but the trunk itself: no venerable elm
or oak, perhaps; but prince in my own realm.

Gerald Mangan

Eddie in Paris
pen and ink drawing

Poor Old Eddie Linden
a Lanarkshire skipping-song.

Eddie Linden broke his jaw
Drinkin' Irish whisky raw.
He blamed it on the ice and snaw.
Poor old Eddie Linden.

Eddie always breaks the ice
When parties lack a bit of spice.
He never gets invited twice.
Poor old Eddie Linden.

Eddie Linden broke the rules
Behind the cycle-shed at school,
Soliciting a Papal Bull.
Poor old Eddie Linden.

Eddie Linden broke a rib
Marching for 'Gay Gordons' Lib'.
He went and shouted 'Up the Hibs'.
Poor old Eddie Linden.

Eddie Linden broke a tooth
Telling Pastor Glass the truth.
He bit the glass and cut his mooth.
Poor old Eddie Linden.

Eddie nearly broke his skull
When Larkin asked him up to Hull.
He said 'Yer books are awfy dull.'
Poor old Eddie Linden.

When Eddie's underneath the sod,
They'll kick him up the stairs to God
For calling Lucifer a Prod.
Poor old Eddie Linden.

Gerda Mayer

Knock-Knees, Bow-Legs

Knock-Knees, Bow-Legs,
danced together, danced together.
Let us marry. Our child
shall reform us altogether.
Straight-limbed Sure-Foot
stood up, strode the world round.
But it was their jaunty capers
jumped his parents off the ground.

Eddie arriving at the gate of heaven
pen and ink drawing

Gerald Mangan

John Montague

TELL THEM, JOHN
or A QUESTION OF IDENTITY

Crossing a leafy Cambridge quad
with three brilliant French poets
(Deguy, Marteau, Roubaud)
we are dogged by a tow-headed
and insistent Eddie Linden.

'Tell them, John, that I'm homosexual.'
'*Il dit qu'il est homosexuel*,'
I dutifully tell my friends, who
nod with puzzled politeness, '*Ah, oui*?'
but do not seem surprised.

'Tell them, John, that I'm a bastard.'
'*Il dit qu'il est bâtard*,' and
they nod their sage heads again…
Eyes glinting beneath his red beret,
Eddie charges in, for the *coup de grâce*.

'Tell them, John, that I'm a homosexual
Catholic bastard, from Glasgow.'
'*It est un bâtard homosexuel*
catholique écossais,' I sigh.
Deguy halts, aghast. '*Et aussi poète*?

Mais c'est pire que Rimbaud
descendant de Charleville!'
I look hard at Eddie. 'He says
your plight is worse than Rimbaud
fleeing to Paris from Charleville.'

*'He says he's a manic-depressive alcoholic lapsed-Catholic
Irish working-class pacifist-communist bastard, from Glasgow.
And would you like to subscribe to a poetry magazine.'*

Mary Montague

'Unskilled at art or verse...'

Unskilled at art or verse
I struggle to impart,
A graphic image
Of you, sitting at my window table
Eating an Ulster fry; or
Sharing words with friends, come
To celebrate another May marked year.

And the power of the talk is great
And words make flesh our youth
The quick and the dead are one
Hampstead and Kilburn
Earl's Court and Maida Vale
The M1 to Glasgow; Toronto and New York
All figure in the 'crack'.

The role of the poet is lauded, if feared
And bardic traditions recalled.
Religion, literature, politics, life
Compete for the bitter tongue.
But in the post-noon sun
We break bread and drink the vine
With friends, who dig with the other foot.

We map our years with his;
And in the ghosts of evening
Others join our feast,
No need of turned-down glass.
Three score years and ten
In the age of *Aquarius*, elections mark this day
For Bessie Glackin's famous son.

Stop

an anti-war poem for Eddie

Urgent talks having broken down, the peace will be intensified
through war. These are safe bombs, and any fatalities
will be minors. The targets are strictly military
or civilian. Until our aim is achieved we will continue
missing. Anomalies may recur, but none
out of the ordinary. This release has been prepared by
official Stop

First reports indicate a major break through
hospital roofs. The bombs were strictly targeted at
personnel. The hated dictatorship is over
the moon. Any errors are a mere blip
on the radar screen. We anticipate a stepping up
of funerals. Reporters are free to file copy
which we Stop

We can confirm that many personnel now enjoy peace,
underground. Several terrorist leaders have been
created overnight. In modern war, mistakes are never made
official. Our smart bombs are subject only to
intelligence errors. Certain one-off tragic events
will regrettably recur. There are no reporting restrictions
other than Stop

In another time-zone, the bombs fall unsafely.
There are reports of urgent talk under the rubble.
Countless children lie unaccounted for in morgues.
Events are strictly dictated by random dictators.
Regrettably, we are unable to offer regrets today.
This poem has been subject to certain restrictions.
Stop.

Andrew Motion

From the Balcony

The other, smaller islands we can see
by turning sideways on our balcony -

the bubble-pods and cones, the flecks of green,
the basalt-prongs, the moles, the lumpy chains -

were all volcanoes once, though none so tall
and full of rage for life as ours, which still

parades its flag of supple wind-stirred-smoke
as proof that once day soon it will awake

again and wave its twizzle-stick of fire,
demolish woods, block roads, consume entire

communities with stinking lava-slews
which seem too prehistoric to be true

but are. Or will be. For today we sit
and feel what steadiness the world permits.

The metal sun hangs still, its shadows fixed
and cowering. The oily sea-smell mixed

with thyme and oleander throws a drape
as palpable as mist across the drop

of roofs and aerials, of jigsaw-squares,
of terraced streets side-stepping to the shore,

of bathers sprawling on the stones, of waves
like other bathers turning in their graves,

and there, beyond them in the blistered shade
below the mountain, of the giant bird -

no, bi-plane, with a bucket slung beneath -
which sidles idly in to drench a wreath

of bush-fire in the fields, a fire that we
suppose means nothing to us here, but have to see.

The Mountain Is Holding Out

The mountain is holding out
for news from the sea
and the raid on the redoubt.
The plain won't level with me

for news from the sea
is harder and harder to find.
The plain won't level with me
now it's non-aligned

and harder and harder to find.
The forest won't fill me in
now it too, is non-aligned
and its patience wearing thin.

The forest won't fill me in
nor the lake confess
to its patience wearing thin.
I'd no more try to guess

why the lake might confess
to a regard for its own sheen,
no more try to guess
why the river won't come clean

on its regard for its own sheen
than who you and I've faced across a ditch.
For the river not coming clean
is only one of the issues on which

you and I've faced across a ditch
and the raid to redoubt
only one of the issues on which
the mountain is holding out.

'Ranged, fanned as in the apocalypse...'

Ranged, fanned as in the apocalypse,
Those who were not defiled, the victims,
Children, great-aunts, lacemakers and especially
The laborious foreigners, every one
Bearing the emblem of his trade,
They are captured listening to the lines
That hold and tangle, trapping their lives
In a room upstanding with white pedestals and busts
And a plain, good carpet (there will be coffee soon).
The verses halt and tug. Why do they allow it,
Are they bullied or too modest, can they feel honoured
By the partial mugshot? Here is the coffee,
And probably whiskey in the far parlour
For the famous who stand and stretch.
                                        And I spot you, Eddie,
Stepping back from the spillage,
Imprisoned against glass bookcases
Where rows of spines slide from *Assyrian* to *Hittite*
(No script more strange, no dragon a more
Outrageous presence than yours) and you draw breath
Because your retreat is partial, and when you speak
A draught from a city of broken windows
Will come razoring under the door.

Vocation

Vocation varies, where we tend to prodigal,
How we take and give our own example:
The Occident, the Orient, or both:
Whether or not to cut our personal cloth.

Initiation grants us place among
Like aspirants. We each chant our song
While we keep faith; may mature to hymn.
Some stay in choir. The rest change voice, go dumb.

As postulants we've time to meditate
Upon our choice of life and to collate
What was left, what taken. Both texts evaluated
We may decide to stay, or change our mind.

With ordination we apply what's learned
From the contents and consecrate what's miracled.
Some may scripture what inspires vocation,
To sacrament its value and its duration

Brian Patten

for Eddie on his birthday

God Bless the Poor?

I keep seeing the phrase 'God bless the poor.'
Who first wrote it down —
That ultimate cop-out,
the most perfectly passed buck in history —
passed on and on till it lands
far off in the cosmos,
on God's desk where we need pay it no attention?
'God bless the poor'
It's found everywhere —
Scraped on pyramids,
Cast in runes, writ in gold script in churches,
on pompous memorials,
on drinking fountains in municipal gardens —
It runs like a pious stream of piss through history —
'God bless the poor'
Did the poor scratch it themselves on pyramids?
Did they crawl through the vaulted churches on bleeding knees
in order to write it?
And did Jesus really say it?
Maybe him with pale skin and blue eyes
maybe that fraud,
But Jesus?
No, it's likely to be a bad translation,
Or a cunning adaptation made
By the early owners of Language & Co.
Maybe it ought to have been
'God inspire the poor'
or
'God inflame the poor'
But not
'God bless the poor',
No, never that!
For all that phrase does is pass on the buck
While the poor wait
Passive, on their knees, heads bowed humbly,
Perfectly positioned for the beheading.

Long Time Back, A Guilt

Dinna betray me!

was it in Edinburgh
dear Eddie
or the Guildhall in Derry
I heard you cry out?
and saw you – king of the sheughs
and the ditchbacks
another bare Sweeney –
as with only one invite
I jeuked into a party
a big warm jostly party
lots of drink and ould crack
but I left you there out-
with the rush – as ever anxious
eager and unappeased

Peter Porter

for Eddie Linden's 70th

State of the Art

Another century of inequality —
To what forecasts will that equate?
The Abolition of Child Poverty?
Great wealth and petitioners at the gate?
A website for each incivility?
State of the Art becomes Art of the State?

Eddie, you have known it all along
And fought to keep faith with humanity —
And judged Art mattered, that poetry belonged
With Social Justice, nothing touchy-feely,
No glib absconding to the moneyed throng,
A Sane Mind questioning New Insanity.

Bagdad

Chruinnigh dhá mhíle file Súifeach i mBagdad aréir
Piléir is roicéid is gránáidí á scaoileadh
Ach níor chuala Allah ach a bhfíonghuth siúd
An fhilíocht amháin a chuaigh caol díreach ina caor
thine go Parthas naofa
Na buamaí is na pléascáin go léir
Shoilsíodar an náire, tamall,
Gur thum de gheit go talamh

Sileann macalla a mbriathra trí chneácha

Baghdad

Two thousand Sufi poets assembled in Baghdad last night
Bullets, rockets and grenades flying
Allah heard only their wine voices
Bursting in a fireball straight to Paradise
Bombs and explosives
Illuminated the shame for an instant
Before sinking suddenly to earth

Echoes of their words seep through wounds

Anthony Rudolf

Eddie at George Barker's funeral London 1991

John Minihan

Unter Den Linden

Well, they are gone, and here must I remain,
this lime-tree bower my prison, and the name
of the avenue a trigger for my thoughts
about the places where our paths would cross:

Indica, Turret, Voice Box, Lamb and Flag,
and now friends' funerals. Only last week,
we shook hands at the crematorium
in Hoop Lane (home to the ashes of the man

whose hyper-real sculpted image freaked
first-time visitors to Turret Bookshop),
and said goodbye with Horovitz and Brownjohn
to 'Barnet Finkelstoen', Bernard Stone.

You recalled I'd brought you Rabbi Hugo Gryn's
book to read in hospital, and I tell you
Hugo's buried across the road, escort you
to the Jewish cemetery, a 'stoen's' throw

from Bernard's coffin, to inspect the grave
of this man you admired fiercely. And now
for thee, my gentle-hearted Eddie, *to whom*
no sound is dissonant which tells of life,

talk of my gift — before our friend was ashes —
was a reminder you'd survived the knife,
that we are guests at a life-long party thrown,
some say, by the Almighty, Lord of Hosts.

So, drink to life until our bullet's numbered
and may the Lord have mercy on our ghosts.
But not yet, Eddie Linden, always first
with the news, bursting in on Nuttall's reading,

to announce that Ezra Pound had died:
'We've all moved up one, then,' he replied.
In the firing line, who's next? *And now*
my friends emerge / beneath the wide wide heaven.

Elegy For Eleanor Young, and 1965

'There are no sexual madeleines'
GRAHAM GREENE

'Don't wake the Tarkington ghosts.'
F. SCOTT FITZGERALD

So young your shoulders of snow burn with roses,
Your opium-black electric long hair
Flies as your sex exults, expends inverted velvets.
Come settle in spools from the shock;
Our shared Egyptian cigarette
Exhales in post-coital peals of laughter.

Your scent of sandalwood stays
Embedded in my sweater.
How many years is this
You brush your macaw mane to Blonde on Blonde?
Eleanor of the Lowlands,
With dark eyes disavowing
Your musk that unmakes derangements,
Your cool-warm complex voice of modern jazz.

By your throat's demure brown ribbon
Enfolding time and space
Party-lights this Christmas eve dance in your silver cross.
You cross the room and kiss me for a dare –
Or poetry, my petty youthful "fame"? -
You take me to myself in you, affirm a cool white flame
Whose mystery spills inward from our lips
In tongues, your silk saliva's tone of rose;
My embouchure implores
The new reed of your sex.
In midnight mass your fingers flute my sleeve.
With your coat of chocolate suede
Unbuttoned to permit

Bernard Saint

My hand to slip
Come lie in my lap like a cat,
For this conversation finds our feet entwined
Let us close our eyes on hubristic
Reason and kiss;
The archetypal realm
Draws in like candlelight.

In a dream you bring me a bush;
Its leaves, inscribed with Hebrew letters,
Read together ring like a bell.
Take me to your inglenook
Moonlit Spanish Zohar rug,
To the congress of the dove
Where lovers don't "make" love
But love descends
Melting Zurich melancholic gold
Financial world-control
Into fierce seraphic infinite light.

With your coffee-house eyes and your claret velvet dress,
With your chalice mouth oblique and Dylanesque,
With the warm wine of your mouth in the Northwest rain,
With the grail of your mind's design,
With your words flown south on a warehouse wind
                    Engels marvels you inspire
                    No velvet revolution.

Give yourself to me that I
Preserve you whole – so lovers say
In human fallibility;
Take off the gospel which you wear
Like columbine. Combine
Empirical and numinous intensity.

Eye to eye — 'A Love Supreme' — we lean into a booth:
The Record Shack in twilight market town.
The double-bass motifs bring down a clean cymbal rain

Brighid McLoughlin

Portrait of Eddie
Pen and ink drawing

Bernard Saint

The epicentre hurls its meaning home:
Antidiamorphine. You are my John Coltrane;
Sober total recall in spiritual sheets of sound.

Sister Rosetta Tharpe and Otis Spann
Stand on Stockport Station so bemused;
Arlo Guthrie strolls with me through apathy and Crewe;
A confluence of folk-blues-poetry;
Ferlinghetti reads on prime TV.
Hitching from Andalusia, Eddie Linden
Enters The Turk's Head, Salford, clad
In kilt and tam o shanter.
'He's only sixteen,' he shouts as I read —
As I go to buy drinks at the bar.
His pointed face-bones burn, bright orange hair,
Impetuous energies,
A Cassidy sans Cadillac, so hot-wired
He vibrates.
A set of spokes and sparks in search of a wheel,
A set of angles poised to find a hinge,
Immanent profound point of connection;
Who has suffered departures now demands arrival;
In empty Cheshire lanes he shouts for taxis.

He describes himself Scots-Irish-Roman-Catholic
Homosexual-Socialist-CND;
I think he is Jewish-Gregarious-Lonely, and from this
Builds poetry's equivalence of Crewe Station,
Changing three generations onto democratic trains
Of readings, parties, Aquarian magazines.

It is 1965. Beyond the brown light of your eyes
The world turns psychodelinquent.
Conservative lysergic generation
Fuddy-duddy Beatle-bands pop-minimise psychosis.

Pete Brown admires a partial line of mine –
" In my White Room with black curtains…." Soon becomes
Cream's brown compound : smacks of constipation.
Kerouac contesting on TV
"In a little church Sainte-Jeanne-d'Arc.
I whispered beat, be-at, Beatitude…
A Dionysian movement I did not intend,
Concerned instead with order, tenderness –
Yes, it was pure in heart."

Kingdom of heaven untaken by force;
You kiss me in the country church,
I caress you and you come
Standing shaking fully-clothed
Shouting all is holy.
Flowers of the summer field,
Fair love and sacred knowledge,
Unfurl their mild mandalas
Patiently within the mind's true breath.
With you I wake in Lowell and am blessed.

Oedipal hate in masquerade of universal love,
A cultural renaissance may not rise
From reefer-pads' regressive daisy-chains;
Sensation' style and surface entertain
Souls habitually denying shadow:
Pseudo-adults batten on the young,
Promote the Human Be-In; Nuremberg.

Your Cocteau radio jump-cuts linear time;
Warm valves bloom within Tristano's tale –
Amber-laden lines of cubist cool –
Billy Bauer's D'Angelico guitar.
" Sange de Poete" is the only station;
Hebraic-Aramaic cantors there
Contemporise advice to who will hear –
"There is a line between love and fascination
Lost to an Age such as this…"

Then sing like a lark
High to be home
Daughter in Zion

By your profile of pearl
By your blues silhouette
Refute on fire
Darwinian rule
And see the world as a mystical work.
The carnival draws to a close

But for the fireworks' pastel orchestration –
A sympathetic magic moving in
Imperceptibly and unexpected,
Reminds you of Sinatra's "Where or When";
Kerouac-in-Lowell listens in;
Tender is the night in leafy Hulme.
Scott Fitzgerald's cardiac occlusion
Leaves " The Last Tycoon" to hang in mid-air
Development of a girl named Eleanor.

Scott's friend Phelps Puttman's verse " The Rose"
Prefigures Dr. Jung's work on addiction;
From the bottom of his bourbon brand "Three Roses"
He's turned in his delirium towards The Mystic Rose.
The Sad-Eyed Lady of the Lowlands
I doubt is Sarah Lowndes.

Time regained; its mystery attained
Whose price is innocence.
Clocks cast off their silver crowns,
Seed-clock crowns of dandelion
In summer snowflakes veil your face.
You trickle sand upon my palm,
The desert feeds me honey.

Shepherd my Gretsch guitar to the fold in your arms,
Your delicate brow descending
Into a haze of jet and July spangles.
"Harvest your words of love," you sing
As I gather you to my arms
Lie silk wheat like water
As you run down
Your chord progression called "The Wildwood Flower"

As you run down.
As time runs as I gather you as you run
From time to timelessness gone
Into the One
Whose centre is everywhere, circumference nowhere,

Eleanor is done?
Eleanor, Arise now, Eros is a Rose

Little Magazines

Hungry red-wristed
Keepers of the true
Small unsentimental tone
Or thread or litmus paper
That in the midst of madness
Or chaos or revolution
(When passions obscure
And everyone repudiates
What he knew)
Steadily sturdily
Keep a small-sized
Truth in view
(Small-sized is
The embryo too):
Them I salute
Because we can't go out on a limb
Without guardians
Like them.
Eddie Linden, for instance,
Let us hymn.

The Hincks Version 1847

'I am very sure that there is a strong feeling in some influential quarters that I must be kept out of the field of discovery, whatever may occupy it. I am now laid on the shelf; and I never expect to have again the means of pursuing my discoveries.' Edward Hincks, Killyleagh

'I look upon Dr Hincks as the first discoverer of the Assyrian language.'
William Henry Fox Talbot, 1861, letter to Julius Oppert

Meanwhile, she bore the girl on her own back for three days those six miles.
Will it be believed? On Dundrum strand, the *Great Britain* is still on its side,
a palace of cables and masts and pianos and perishable goods,

an empire ploughed back into the sand, a colossal wreck. After eight months,
the novelty of the impossible having taken place already is wearing thin,
for all Brunel himself had come, his fat cigar smoking and his top hat like a fat cigar,

another dwarf among the monsters famine let loose among the dunes
to stare and beg and disappoint like Egyptians and Persians and Greeks of that age,
stupid among monuments, knowing neither who built them nor how they spoke.

Of course, as soon as they reached the infirmary, her daughter died.
Of disease. Of rust on the skin. Of a tongue big as a gourd.
Meanwhile, in Killyleagh the stern Assyrian surgeons advance relentlessly

over the sheets in the Rector's study now his ladies have left (rock cakes on lace).
Their clay headdresses are as square and stiff as sails or their own grey faces.
A gaze fixed still on the disc of the sun as flat as earth, nothing turns their heads or his.

Certainly not suffering. Certainly not that tableau of two women carved into the moment,
concubines, perhaps, unfortunates of a warrior nation. And so is lost forever
what he is searching for, among the tiny skeletons the words of a language leave,

among the bird's-feet scamperings, among the marks a dove might leave
lighting on mud-flats when waters subside. Something beached like death itself.
Something massive. Overbearing. Irresistibly finite. A determinative. An adverb. An ark.

Matthew Sweeney

Coming Home

He crossed the sea in a coracle
to show it could be done.

The coracle was made of pigskins
stretched over pig bones

and held most of the rest of the pig
in stews, salamis, and hams.

He had a paddle, a sail, a motor
and a bottle of Talisker,

a walkman primed with Latin jazz,
a translation of the Inferno,

a photo of a topless woman,
a lifebelt, a flare-gun, a revolver.

On his head he wore a headdress
of green parrot feathers

and on his body was a wetsuit
under an Afghan coat.

As he approached the Irish coast
he flew the tricolour

and as he veered for the pier
he stood up and saluted

the statue at the harbour mouth,
while whistling the Soldier's Song.

This earned him a few shouts
from a staggering drunk

and cheering and clapping
from a gang of smoking girls.

He bowed, lassoed the capstan,
and hauled himself onto Ireland.

Ode for Eddie

When I first came to London
Aged seventeen
I might have met Eddie Linden —
But this could not have been,
For he was up in Glasgow
And as the grass is green
We went by different highways —
Bu O the things we've seen.

And O the things in glasses
Put into our lips,
As year by year time passes
And, much like passing ships,
We met and drank and chatted
Fuddled with too much booze
Till the host waved us homeward —
But O the things we lose

In idleness and insult
Outstaying what began
As golden promises and exult-
ation. 'The tree of man
Was never quiet' — good old Housman
'Give me your arm, old toad' —
Larkin would send his greetings
As Eddie hits the road

Onto the final stretch,
Where we shall find *Aquarius*
Carrying his cans of water,
And Charon will gently carry us
Over the dark Styx
To the blessed shores beyond us
Where all poems end,
Immaculate, round the bend.

Trevor Tolley

for Eddie Linden at 70

A Backward Glance of a 'Golden Ager'

Mr MacGregor
You're dead

you used to give us 'the latest gen'
At your Air Raid post in Hitler's war
Chomping your guff while incendiaries fell

West Indians drive the buses now
Where the 48 tram used to run;
And mini-vans cruise past
The old Toc H club

— condemned

Like you

(like both of us)

Mr MacGregor

No epiphany today
Where pensioners queue with shopping and free passes
Homing for supper in a jumble of nostalgia.

(Note: "gen" = Information.
OED: "slang. abbrev….for the
general information of…").

Van Gogh in Brixton

In Hackford Road SW 9,
there is a house where Van Gogh lived:
there is of course the high, blue plaque,
but more importantly, the woman who lives there
has placed a vase of dried sunflowers in the window;

A nice touch that,
the blue plaque,
the sunflowers,
a little bit of green attracting sunlight
into a city garden.

Yet across the road at the school where I teach
— and the woman cleans —

There is a bunker
where the school keeper, keeps coal.

Note: It was after this brief and apparently happy sojourn in Hackford Rd, that the young Vincent set off for the Flemish coal mines, to one of the unhappiest periods of his life. I choose this poem to celebrate Eddie because of his Van Gogh like fervour, his messianic desire to propagate poetry and extend the reach of his beloved magazine, *Aquarius*. S.T.

Charles Walsh

Stone

I could have, should have
passed you by
but something in that strange morphology
caught the slanted eye,
trapped within that gaping jaw, unwanted
stone within a stone,
aliens on an alien shore.
How many tides, how many waves
have washed you down the years?
How many more must break
upon your furrowed brow
and set you free
upon your ceaseless wandering
to some unknown finality
in yet another sea?

Stones do not belong
are always from.
Torn from the furnace of time,
worn old by wind and wave, ice and rain,
rock, stone, pebble, sand —
the certain regression into the primal slime
from whence we came.

Sometimes they skim like silver shadows
on dark flat water
or lie in deeper pools
where fishes hide their young
and predators wait alone.

Alone.
But that was in another land
where stones still persecute, torment, or maim.
There stone is cold and hard
upon the withered hand,
cracks the shovel, blunts the spade.
The young, already stooped,
the old, hunched, or broken backed,
from under moss drenched walls
watch wearily as stones begin to grow again
in weedy fields where crops too often fail.

Black against the fading light
lone sentinels of the winter gods
cast their shadows deep into the distant dark
of the ancient art.
The blood of heroes inscribed in
words half formed, forgotten or unread.
yet still they stand defiant
upon the mouldering ground
where broken axe and rusted sword
lie buried with their warrior dead.

All night stones rattle in your head,
screams half heard,
the empty tomb,
fragments of the stonebird's cry
embedded in an older pain
now passed within the passing rain.

I walk upon the empty strand.
They will not return.

Above, beyond wherever they are gone or lain
the unendying sky remains.

Joseph Woods

Tyrekicking

There might be a halting somewhere east
of Drumshanbo where the small talk
is of angle grinders, carburettor-crankshafts
and bent axles, and if I knew the form,

I wouldn't make strange, lounging outside
a garage in overalls, tyrekicking the days
away and knowing the pedigree of every
passing vehicle. Leaning expertly to each

new arrival on the forecourt, I'd sometimes
straighten my back and nose the wind for change.
While the radio, oily as a discarded car-battery,
would blabber on the hour with news of the world.

Macdara Woods

for Eddie

From The April Roads Of Longford

I've been hearing
the marvellous names:
bloodworm butterworth
sphagnum moss —

Been remembering a child
filling up bottles
to hear the sounds —
in the stream
at the end of my grandmother's haggard:

The *bop-bop-bop-bop-bop*
on a rising scale
air and water trading places —
colours of sound and glass
and each one different:

I feel the water and mud
and rising warmth
the flowing puddle
we called a river
me crouched in colour and sound:

And that's what April said —
wherever it is
that far off place
that keeps us here:
how we keep going back to where we are

Alwyn Gillespie

Male Nude
pen and ink drawing

prose and remininiscences

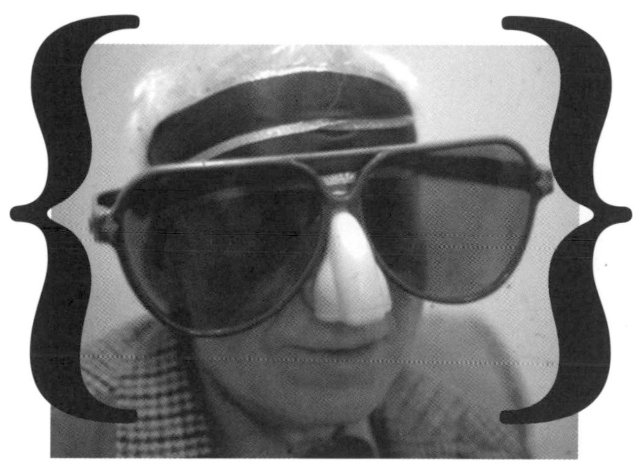

I know 2 who deserve to be called true servants of the servants of Art, & Eddie, one is you - says Alasdair - also liking you being a working-class homosexual Catholic Socialist intellectual
originally drawn by A. Gray 1989, redrawn 2005
FOR of such is the KINGDOM of HEAVEN

Dermot Ahern

I first met Eddie fifteen years ago or so through my cousin Constance Short whom he has visited in Ireland since 1968.

He is a hard man to label – the description often bandied about such as 'cultural entrepreneur', 'the last bohemian', really don't do justice to the complexity and depth of the man.

One Saturday a couple of years ago I came across a poem called 'Incident in Exeter Station' by Matthew Sweeney in The Guardian newspaper. Reading through it I remember the appeal of the central character – a difficult, unique sort of man. I came to the bottom of the page and found the words; '*Dedicated to Eddie Linden*' I laughed and tore out the cutting. It conjures him up – restless, cheeky, bold, intelligent and intense – the Celt abroad. I found him to have a great sense of humour too.

To be honest, I am not a major poetry fan. I can, however, readily appreciate Eddie's ability to paint so many layers, colours and intensities of emotion in so few words and lines. The six short lines of 'The Miner' is a case in point.

No doubt, it is Eddie's own abilities and experience as a poet which have led him to give so much of his time and talents to supporting other poets. In a world where the arts are often denigrated and undervalued, people like Eddie are more necessary than ever. It's 36 years since the first issue of *Aquarius* appeared in 1969 and through a 'series of minor miracles' is still going today. Long may his efforts last – one of the few of us who has really made a difference! Happy 70th Birthday Eddie from Maeve and me.

Alasdair Gray

Portrait of Eddie, 2005
pen and ink drawing

Jonathan Barker

'There are not many men...'

There are not many men like Eddie Linden. Indeed there are not. Eddie is classless and, as a mutual friend told me recently, 'without a mean bone in his body'. He is the same intense — but essentially amiable — person whenever we meet. A sensitive person with a curiously old-fashioned sense of courtesy and a manner by turns thoughtful and animated. He treats everyone the same be they a young poet or a Lord. I have met him with both. Attend a poetry book launch in London or elsewhere and there is Eddie, always engaged in discussion, soon to wander over and warmly ask after my family.

From 1973 into the later 1980s I was Librarian of the Arts Council Poetry Library in London. We were based, in the early days, in a long thin room in London's Piccadilly approached through marble portals that opened into a splendid 18th century interior with a bust of Lord Goodman in the hall. Into this calm world flowed an ever-growing crowd of poets, small press and little magazine publishers and a very diverse group of poetry readers. Walking along Piccadilly one evening I met a lively man, walking and talking faster than anyone I had met before...Eddie Linden. Together we marched up Piccadilly to a party at the Arts Council Shop in Sackville Street. Eddie is a part of the last of the Soho world of writers and artists and I met many with him at this time in the Museum Tavern, the French Pub, or a cavernous pub below Piccadilly Circus called Ward's Irish House – now long closed - which served the best Guinness in London.

There are few rewards in editing a magazine such as *Aquarius* and we have to wonder at the dedication of a man who has produced so many issues over so many years. Literary magazines have a vital role in introducing a new generation of writers to readers and we all need to be grateful to *Aquarius* for achieving this. But *Aquarius* has been influential, too, in publishing new work by some of the most individual and distinguished poets of our time. Poets such as John Heath-Stubbs, David Wright, David Gascoyne, George Barker, W.S. Graham. The critical standing of these writers is higher today than at any other time and I am certain that *Aquarius* has played a major role in helping this important and just evaluation to come about.

Christmas with Eddie

Eddie spent Christmas with my family since before I was born. Eddie reminds me of my mother's generosity; Constance took in the adult 'orphan' for over thirty years.

Thank you Eddie for bringing a world of mystery, imagination and fun with you in the illustrated children's books you brought for Christmas. They have been treasured.

Thank you also for the much loved teddy bears you named Lesley and Borris. Lesley was a soft panda given to me and Borris a coarse haired brown bear for my brother Finn.

The only piece of poetry I learned from Eddie was:
"Eddie Lindie, broke a windie on a Sunda mornin, the polis came and took his name and made him say good morning".

Nessa Behan
aged 8 months with
Seán Hutton, Eddie Linden
and Constance Short. Dublin Zoo,
Christmas 1974.
Photograph: John Behan

Gordon Bowker

Eddie Linden — A Memoir

It was in the mid-1960s, while living in a Chelsea bed-sitter, that I first met young Eddie. Douglas Hyde, ex-Communist-turned-Catholic journalist, suggested I contact him, saying that he was about to launch a poetry magazine, *Aquarius*. Having poetic pretensions at that time, I thought I might find an outlet for my feeble verse.

All I can recall of our first encounter is of us drinking the night away and talking endlessly. Eddie, an amiable dynamo full of gossip, apparently knew every poet in town. Perhaps that was the occasion that I mentioned a beautiful girlfriend who had once lived with an artist called Bill Redgrave in a studio behind Finch's pub in the Fulham Road.

'I know Bill,' said Eddie, 'Let's pay him a visit.'

I pointed out that it was well after midnight, but Eddie was now feeling convivial and just 'knew' that Bill would welcome us like long lost brothers.

We staggered along the Fulham Road to the mews behind the pub and found Bill's studio. He was probably asleep but eventually responded to our hammering and very decently invited us in for a drink.

Then occurred a disaster that haunts me still. The floor of Bill's studio was crammed with sculptures, looking rather like that famous terracotta army of Chinese warriors. At some point, needing a leak, I tottered off towards a distant door indicated by Bill, and the inevitable happened. I lurched against one of his statues, which keeled over and smashed into a thousand pieces. I was mortified, but Bill was charming and forgiving and poured yet more whisky. Shortly afterwards the evening ended, leaving me with a story I forever associate with first meeting Eddie.

I reviewed some poetry for early *Aquariuses*, which I still have — collectors' items today, I imagine. Then its editor and I lost touch. I fell among academics and betrayed the muse, while he remained faithful to her.

We met again thirty years later — again through Douglas Hyde. Eddie, I thought, had changed little — still the amiable dynamo — except that now he was a celebrity, the subject of a book known to readers of poetry throughout the metropolis and beyond. I was invited to see the play *Who is Eddie Linden?* and watched it sitting beside the hero/the poet observing his doppelganger. It was a strange flashback to the 60s, but re-enacting a parallel life I'd been unaware of.

I wrote again for *Aquarius* – a review of Robert Fraser's biography of George Barker, *The Chameleon Poet.* Barker's world was Eddie's world — pub, poetry readings, the vortex of literary gossip news from Bohemia — a scene long gone. Or is it? Perhaps it's still there but known only to those who know where to find it. Eddie may be the one who holds it all together, the man at the centre, still on visiting terms with ghosts of Barker, Maclaren-Ross, Francis Bacon, the Barnard brothers, Bill Redgrave, Hamish Henderson, and the whole riotous company. I hope so. He deserves his place in Bohemia's Poet's corner.

James Campbell

Sage of Aquarius

One of the more interesting things about my life is that I was once barred from Abbotsford in Edinburgh, in a case of mistaken identity involving Eddie Linden. As the charge hands called for last orders, I was sleepily opting out of a conversation with some friends, while Eddie went the rounds of the pub's other customers and helped himself to their drinks. It so happened that Eddie and I were wearing the same coloured jacket that night, and when I entered the Abbotsford the following evening, it was to be greeted with the baneful words: "You're Barred". Only after a long period of exile to the draughty halls of the Café Royal did I succeed in convincing the Abbotsford barmen that I was not Eddie Linden. Eddie was suitably embarrassed about my predicament, but I couldn't help feeling that he was relieved that it was, after all, mine and not his. The last thing that I saw the night I was ordered out was Eddie at the other end of the bar emptying a glass of Guinness down his throat. Eddie is the most vulnerable person that I have ever met. He's so tender and raw, it's as if he has no skin. Almost every conversation with him comes round to the subject of who he is, how the hell could God go and dump on him like this? The thing that has literally saved his life is *Aquarius*. There are no synonyms in the English language, but "Eddie" and "Aquarius" , come close. The times when he has come nearest to answering the question, Who is Eddie Linden? are when a new issue of *Aquarius* has just come off the press. Then Eddie, editor and publisher, blooms, and the answer to the question is suddenly clear: Eddie is the man God put on earth to edit a poetry magazine.

There is no denying that Eddie can be a difficult character. An evening that kicks off with the puritanical Eddie Jekyll, who would no more swear in front of a lady than he would torture a kitten, can end well into injury time with Eddie Hyde condemning all manner of hypocrites and poetasters to everyone within earshot. There was a time now past, when Eddie could empty a room quicker than anyone. Many a literary London figure has ducked into a doorway on catching sight of Eddie down the long Soho street. But as his close friend and biographer Sebastian Barker says, "Eddie notices everything". Sure enough, he can be like a child, picking up more than the grown-ups give him credit for- more, even, than the grown-ups.

I've always thought that you can tell a lot about someone's character from seeing how they react to Eddie. He once interrupted the late American poet Robert Creeley at a reading in Cambridge with shouts from the gallery: " Gwan yersel', Bob! Gie these young Cambridge students a lesson." Creeley used to read so softly it was almost a mumble, so this might have been thought likely to displease him, but his next book contained a poem dedicated to Eddie. More than anything, he appreciates loyalty, and will put up with the odd snapped "Eddie, behave yersel", if confident of its essential good nature.

In February 1995, a play deriving from Sebastian Barker's book opened at a small theatre near the Angel, Islington, starring Michael Deacon as Eddie, and featuring a series of arguments, apologies and near-intimate encounters between him and a young poet, whose burning ambition, it seemed, was to have his poems published in *Aquarius*.

On opening night, Eddie was suffering from an outbreak of stage fright – as if it was he who had to go on stage and play Eddie Linden, rather than Michael Deacon. I had arranged to meet him in a pub downstairs from the theatre an hour before curtain, but as I made my way from the tube I met Eddie in the street, looking worried, superhumanly worried. No one can look worried the way Eddie can. We could have staged the play right there and called it " Eddie Linden is Unwell".

He was dapper, with red carnation and red hankie, but mightly confused. Ever since he discovered, at age of nine, that the woman who had nurtured him was not his real mother, and that his father was nothing, not even a name, he has spent his life trying to find out, "Who is this fellow?" And now as his sixtieth birthday approached, he was he the subject of this curious investigation: a play about him. Over 150 people, mostly known to him, were crowding into the tiny, overheated auditorium to watch another fellah playing at being Eddie Linden – with all his odd expressions of speech and gesture theatricalized – while the real Eddie sat and watched, wondering, Is that what I'm really like? Afterwards, I asked him how he had felt about the performance. "It's just as Burns says: Ye canny see yersel' as others see ye. Well, I just have."

To me, the play failed to catch the poignancy, and the profundity, of the real Eddie.

"It's an exaggerated version of me", Eddie said. Exaggerated? Impossible. I thought it was an understatement. It didn't show what I think of as the real Eddie: a redeeming figure, battling with life on our behalf, facing struggles most of us never have to face and emerging semi-concussed but semi-victorious as well, with an innocent laugh, a childlike trust, a tilt at the Tories, a toast to MacCaig, and, for ever and ever, a new issue of *Aquarius*.

This is a shortened version of an article that first appeared in *The Scotsman.*

Eddie by Starlight

I wake to a loud siren — is it an ambulance? The Fire Brigade? No. It's the phone. It's 4.30AM. 'Hello Mary, it's Eddie, are you awake?' 'I am now Eddie.' 'Oh were you asleep?' 'No! no!'

'Have you a wee pencil? I want you to write down my funeral arrangements. I want 4 Black Horses with plumes drawing my hearse and Harold Pinter, Con Howard and John Behan to be my chief mourners. Seamus Heaney will recite a poem. I want a High Mass. Stop! We'll say a wee haley mary. You sing "Faith of our Fathers". Ah! That's lovely. Now back to the funeral. I want the altar ablaze with candles. I want incense and 20 priests. I want a Latin Mass'

I'm wide awake now, so I might as well enjoy it. 'Eddie, recite "City of Razors".' Eddie bellows into the phone, 'Cobbled streets, littered with broken milk bottles......etc'

I am not alone anymore- London is awake. I place Eddie's instructions on forty similar ones. There's only one Eddie — and that deserves another haley mary.

Elizabeth Chapman (Glackin)

'Ours — a family like so many others...'

Ours - a family like so many others, had little time for diaries, family trees back in the early 20th century and so family history passed on by word of mouth has many personal interpretations.

This is one.
Our paternal grandmother, a young recently widowed Irish woman with four young children left Ireland where there was little means of a livelihood, to come to the west of Scotland to her sister and husband who was fortunate to be employed.

Then, in the 1930's, four grandsons were born all named Edward after her long dead husband, Eddie Linden being the son of the only daughter, Bessie. Eddie was adopted - not by a complete stranger, but into a family, part of the extended family viz. the brother (Linden) of our aunt who was the wife of our uncle Paddy.

A good or a bad thing? A question that can only be answered by Eddie himself. Since my father's two brothers moved south to Corby, England, communication between the families faltered.

So we really only became reacquainted with cousin Eddie when he began working in the steel works, Motherwell, Scotland, where our Dad worked. But Eddie is much more eloquent on this meeting and its aftermath!

Suffice to say, he became a fairly regular visitor to our home — a visitor who often stunned us with his emphatic opinions on religious and political points! Dad was always keen to engage in these exchanges — and often with similar theatrical delivery!

When Dad died on Christmas Day 1989, we contacted Eddie who came from his friends in Ireland without hesitation. Always Eddie has been keen on family — keeping in touch and discovering relatives we knew not at all!

And now, having reached the biblical span of three score and ten, I wish you, Eddie, on behalf of the Glackin family, in the Latin phrase which Dad liked to use on family occasions — *Ad Multos Annos.*

Eddie Linden

I first met Eddie Linden in the summer of 1978 when we were both attending the newly -founded Oxford Literature Festival. I entered a wine-bar just off Cornmarket and saw a small, wiry man with distinctively Celtic colouring (fair skin, auburn hair slightly greying) in sprightly conversation with a man who turned out to be Zbigniew Herbert, my reason for wanting to be at the reading that evening. But soon it was Eddie who focussed my attention by correctly identifying my companion, from the very faintest of burrs, as a Canadian. It was the first evidence that Eddie has a very acute ear for the way others speak and the language they use. Not everyone would guess that behind the broad Glaswegian accent hides a wicked mimic.

The friendship that struck up between us soon showed me that Eddie is indeed multifaceted. When the conviviality is upon him, he will gleefully describe himself as 'a working-class, Catholic homosexual' and he is all of these things. But here is a man from an underprivileged background and upbringing who has been for thirty-five years or more a central figure in the London and Irish literary world: not a predictable path through life. Such a trajectory betokens a character of enormous determination, even doggedness, as anyone knows who has been a guest editor for *Aquarius*, the literary magazine he founded and has run now for a third of a century.

Eddie will persuade the august and the reluctant to contribute material, indefatigably ring and re-ring those who promised to help, chivvy the dilatory editor, search out funds and advertising, make sure that all the disparate and decentralised elements cohere to produce another bumper and often definitive issue of Aquarius.

Eddie's dedication to the seriousness of poetry and its function in society has translated into many other activities as well: he served for many years, sometimes controversially, on the council of the Poetry Society and is regularly to be found in the festivals and pubs of Dublin, Glasgow and Edinburgh — and Toronto — and Paris, where his own work has been rendered into French. But it is especially in his friendships that the particular strength of Eddie's loyalty comes through: he is constantly thinking of how to put people in touch, to make things happen that would not otherwise happen, to establish connections between like-minded writers, to help work into print. Perhaps less well-known is the time he has devoted to friends outside the literary world who have been themselves disadvantaged, ill or disabled; hierarchies of persons do not exist for Eddie. Nor, having known himself the difficulties of being an outsider, does he ever sit in judgment on others unless it be that he catches a whiff of humbug.

To finish: if it is true that we all have our corresponding spiritual animal, then I think Eddie's must be the meerkat: sociable, communicative, always on the lookout for the new, ferreting in corners for a choice morsel and delightedly showing it to the rest of the community, watchful for the dangers of poetic sloth or simulation, wheeling and dealing and bringing on the young.

Happy Birthday, Eddie

Geoffrey Elborn

A Well Justified Sinner

I have often wondered how Eddie would be regarded if he lived in any era other than our own. He might have been transported in the 18th century for his political views, and his declaration of his Catholicism, illegitimacy and homosexuality would not have made a cosy existence, if he could have had one at all. Neither does this 'Scotch poof' fit in 2005 either, but Eddie is a welcome anachronism in this tawdry age. At seventy, he remains steadfastly uncompromising in his views that have remained untainted by the slightest shade of blue. They may make others uncomfortable, for Eddie is a gigantic Scots thistle. Jabbing with an honesty that has no space for pretentiousness, but a stripping back to a pure sense of truth, in his life and work.

It is over fifty years ago that Eddie was driven demented by his background, emotions and circumstances, but paradoxically he needed defeat and ignominy to pile on him until he realized he could use this enforced inferiority as a weapon to expose the real Eddie Linden. No one now needs to ask, 'Who is Eddie Linden?' but if they heard him *roar* 'City of Razors', on the radio, they might wonder if he was a wee hard man, who would not need airwaves for his words to be heard beyond Glasgow's Hope Street.

On a day that the Cardinals have elected a new dinosaur Pontiff, conservative and dangerously orthodox, I thought of one of the finest poems Eddie wrote. His 'Tribute to Archbishop Roberts', a man who '…would not wear temporal power/ Nor rings that glitter in the sun...' reveals the tenderness and sensitive inner Eddie Linden, better than most prose about him can. A poem that hopes that with those like Roberts, the Catholic Church will offer love and the compassionate understanding of the state of today, and not promote a dogma, that judges with a castigating scorn. I can imagine Eddie, after seeing the recent Holy Smoke, ringing up his friends and saying 'Jesus, just look at who we've got! Can you believe it?'

Can I believe that it is over thirty years ago, that I was accosted by Eddie as he trundled a mop and pail in Bernard Stone's Poetry Bookshop in Kensington?

Only for the cause of poetry would I have gone through my pockets to gather coins for a subscription to what was to become *Aquarius*, for I was certainly poorer than Eddie was.

But what a return these few coins bought! An incredible loyalty, a friendship and faith, often undeserved, in my own work when no one else could be bothered to give any encouragement at all.

As Eddie progresses towards his next decade, I hope that, like Roberts, he will find the 'sanctuary and tranquillity' he has earned. Not that Eddie will ever be comfortable, nor would he want to be, for that would betray all the faiths he has kept, and for which we are grateful.

Gerry Harrison

Eddie Linden

In this short passage I will not try to compete with the cast of literary folk or artists ready to place their thoughts about Eddie Linden in a more original manner than mine. These are just moments of a friendship.

I first became immersed in Eddie in The Cruel Sea in Hampstead in 1964. At that time I could manage eight pints of Guinness in an evening and then afterwards we would return to a flat to weep over LPs of Billie Holiday. Eddie always had a slightly manic and preoccupied look, as if he was expecting a tax inspector through the door at any moment. There was a crowd of us — my wife Ellie, Ted and John, Jimmy and Amaryllis, John Heath-Stubbs, David Medalla and his group called The Exploding Galaxy which was a harbinger for the more heady hallucinogenic days of the later 1960s. And no doubt many more, whose names I have forgotten.

Over forty years Eddie has drifted in and out of my life. Sometimes he would return abruptly, with a sudden telephone call but no time for a conversation. Occasionally he would arrive, curmudgeonly and irascible whether on or off the wagon. Often there were copies of *Aquarius* for sale. At all times there was affection.

And then we asked ourselves, of course, 'Who is Eddie Linden?' Who IS he? In his book Sebastian Barker, with Ralph Steadman's clever cover illustration, tries to offer some answers, but the enigma remains. A film-maker at that time, I tried to make a film of the book, but I don't think I would have been any more successful than Sebastian. I really regret that I missed the play at the King's Head because I was working away from London. However I am always reassured that Eddie and I share a love of poetry, politics and Ireland.

I nearly missed Eddie at his 60th birthday party. Was it so long ago? With his permission I had invited my Australian cousin and her sons to the Irish Club to celebrate the big six-o and of course Eddie's successful recovery from serious surgery. He was nowhere to be seen. Just as we thought of leaving he arrived, lurching, and had appeared to forget why we were all gathered at the Irish Club in his name. Nevertheless he received a hero's welcome, as he will no doubt when we see him again.

Best wishes, Eddie.

Con Howard

Unforgettable Eddie

I recall an unforgettable evening with Eddie Linden. Indeed, it is not possible to spend a forgettable evening with him. We came from a party in The Irish Embassy to the Chelsea Arts Club and to The Irish Club in Eaton square to find that in both places Eddie was persona non grata, and indeed there was another – an Irish titled gentleman who shared these honours with him. However, we eventually found a pleasant public house where we had a very enjoyable conversation and we were made welcome. Eddie, of course, had to tell our new found friends that he was "Irish, Catholic, illegitimate and Communist" and he did recite very well his poem "City of Razors". Shortly afterwards we took a plane from London to Shannon to attend The Merriman Summer School in the pleasant Atlantic village of Kilkee in Co. Clare. On the plane he performed a sales miracle by selling copies of *Aquarius* to a large number of Americans – who until then had never heard of *Aquarius*.

When we arrived at the school he was in a very argumentative mood, which annoyed some of the delegates at the school. They asked me, as Director, to get rid of Eddie or they would…into the Atlantic.

One well-known Tory writer said to me that on resigning from the Communist party, in London, his great joy was that he would never have to see Eddie again and he was in shock to find Eddie at the summer school. However, the weather was good and the atmosphere improved and Eddie was made welcome, and he did contribute some fun and charm to the school, before he vanished into other centres in Northern Ireland and Scotland…and that summer is still referred to "as the one Eddie Linden attended".

A Small Proddy

My new jacket and trousers were green. My brother said it was a Pape's colour. The trousers were long. I went through a puddle and the water soaked up my legs. School was at the top of the street then along another yin. We couldnay go that way. The Papes would get us. Their school was in between. They were on the lookout and had piles of stanes. We walked round three other streets. They had Priests in their school. Ye saw them in the playground. Some had big coats. Then too the Nuns, wee women that walked fast. Cloaks covered their heids.

The Papes couldnay pass our school. We had stanes to pelt them. They went down the main road then round by our street and way up there. Ye passed them and saw them looking. Ye knew them if they stayed in yer street and if yez played the gether. Ye gied a secret wee look like a secret wee hullo or else kidded on ye didnay see them.

There were big fights at dinnertime. Boys flung stanes into the playgrounds and the jannies and teachers had to stop it and even sometimes the polis if windies got broke.

Eftir teatime ye were back out and maybe yez played the gether. Then Saturday was the wedding day and ye went to the scrambles. Pape or Proddy didnay matter. When the motor cars drove away men let down the windies and threw out the money. No just boys and lassies. Women were there. If they saw silver coins they stood on them and ye couldnay lift up their shoes. Ye didnay go to faraway Chapels and ye had to be careful at faraway Churches, which boys were there, if they were gauny batter ye.

At the weddings in our street the Papes were okay to see us because it was our street too.. They acted proud. A boy took me into the Chapel and telt me where to sit and I wasnay to talk. They had statues that made ye feart and signs and secret words that were like spells they cast onto ye and if they did ye were in awful trouble. A Proddy couldnay make these signs, even if ye knew what they were. It would go against ye making them or else turn ye into one.

I felt sorry for the boy. He was brave because of all what happened to Papes. I saw him like he was split in two, the bit I knew and the bit that was a Pape. He wore a Necklace. How come? Necklaces were for lassies. Then Candles and Crosses and Holy Water. Proddies didnay have nothing like that. What did we have. We didnay have nothing, no like that. My maw didnay take us to Church. I only went once and it was to get Christened till then I joined the Lifeboys.

Bruce Kent

Eddie with Ben Kiely, Dublin 2001

John Moran

How to sum up Eddie Linden? Poet, political activist, enthusiast, socialist, Catholic, permanent popper-up in odd places... perhaps good friend is the best description.

I have known Eddie for many years and heard about him long before we met. A member of PAX and pioneer of the Catholic Nuclear Disarmament Group, he marched with CND in the 1960s. Then he was famous for red hair and an incomprehensible Glasgow accent.

Later he was to be found selling the *Catholic Worker* to surprised congregations on their way into Westminster Cathedral. When I was chaplain to London University Eddie would pop in with the latest idea at any time of the day and most times of night. The late night visits even included a sudden entry into my bedroom when he started a conversation, once I woke up, sitting on the end of the bed, as if we had just met on a bus.

His clerical contacts were of the highest quality — amongst them Simon Blake, Anthony Ross, and Anthony Cheales of the Dominican order. When he was confined to the Charing Cross Hospital a few years ago, he even had to keep a visitors' book in order to remember all those who had turned up. My name went under that of Lord Longford, and similar luminaries, evidence of Eddie's wide range of friends.

These days we make contact mostly by phone as he unloads the latest piece of news of friend or homophobic foe. Radical, optimistic, energetic: those are still good labels for Eddie as he hits threescore years and ten. We hope for many more birthdays to come.

A room in Linden Excerpt

One day in the dark maze of the yew-hedges Sister Lua, who has arthritis, looks up at him from her wheelchair which he's pushing, and says: Tell me the truth. Don't be modest about it. Are you Nanky Poo?

Since he is a bookish young man it is exciting thing for him to have history living along the corridor. The poet he's reading just before he leaves his room writes that there's a wind blowing, cold through the corridor, a death-wind, the flapping of defeated wings from meadows damned to eternal April. The poet has never seen it, but he could have been writing about this corridor. On its dull green walls, a mockery of the grass and the green leaves of life, the sun never shines. All day and all night the big windows at the ends of the corridor, one at the east wing of the house and one at the west, are wide open and from whichever airt the wind does blow it always blows cold. The rooms on the north side of the corridors are, as one might expect, colder and darker than the rooms on the south side, or would be if their light and heat depended totally on the sun.

Before the nuns got here and turned the place into a convalescent home it was lived in by a family famous for generations for a special brand of pipe tobacco. The old soldier who reluctantly, vociferously fading away in a room on the north side of the corridor, says: This house was built on smoke. Just think of that. Smoke.

The old soldier himself belongs to some branch of the family that emigrated to South Africa and made even more money out of burgundy than the people who stayed at home made out of smoke, and there was always as much soldiering as smoke in the family, and big-game hunting, too, to judge by the fearful snarling mounted heads left behind and surviving, undisturbed by nuns and convalescents, in the entrance hall.

You'll be nice to the old man, won't you, Mother Polycarp had said to him. He'll bore you to death. But he needs somebody to listen to him. He hasn't much longer to talk, in this world at any rate.

So he talks to the old soldier in the evenings and, in the afternoons, to the old priest and historian, dying as methodically and academically as he has lived, checking references, adding footnotes, in a room on the south side of the corridor. At other times he reads in his own room, or has visitors, or wheels Sister Lua's wheelchair in the ample bosky grounds, or leaves the grounds on his own and goes through quiet suburban roads to walk slowly, tapping his stick, in the public park that overlooks, across two walls and a railway, the flat sand and bay. It is not an exciting life, but it's not meant to be.

Marius Kociejowski

Eddie, Me & the Pope

What is it about Eddie that invites abuse? Almost three years ago, after having undergone a serious operation, he phoned me. There was a falling note of mortality in his voice.

'Will I be remembered?' he asked.

'Why, yes, Eddie, of course — '

An audible sigh of relief followed, which allowed me sufficient breathing space to com plete my sentence.

'Although it won't be for your contribution to literature.'

'Oh, Jesus!' he chuckled, as if suddenly recollecting various unmentionables.

Actually what I said wasn't entirely a joke; the driving force in him owes more to sheer force of character than it does to critical perspicuity. His instincts — as they were, say, with Tambimuttu, editor of *Poetry London* — have rarely been anything other than sure. Eddie's got an ear for a fake. Also, as Sebastian Barker demonstrated some years ago in his biographical portrait, Who is Eddie Linden?, he is himself the stuff of literature. There are few people more deserving of a collective literary salute. My own relationship with him extends back to the 1970s when he was on the council of the Poetry Society, when it was situated in Earls Court Square. The Society was rather less sleek and politically correct than it has since become. The plasterwork then was always coming loose somewhere. I won't say those were happy days, but at least there was the possibility of a decent punch-up on the stairs or a sexual rumpus on the committee room table. The sparks flew at times, and that it should have given admittance to a highly inflammable Eddie bespeaks the desirability of extreme danger over dull routine.

We had a mutual friend in the late Audrey Nicholson, who was the best friend to poets I have ever known and who, in the same way certain women walk slowly and umbrellaless through rain, may have been born to that very purpose. She was, in some respects, as uncritical as Eddie, but driven by the same passionate breeze. As one might expect with two Celts, both of them auburn, the relationship was at times a stormy one, and its continuance owed much to Audrey's kinder nature, which, between his occasional spasms of rage, Eddie was always gracious enough to acknowledge. Always he softened at the very mention of her name and he still does. And she, however close to the edge he might have pushed her, always forgave him.

If ever there was discord between Eddie and me — and we did nearly come to blows once, in an Indian vegetarian restaurant, where, as I recall, the very atmosphere simpered of peace — it was because of my Polish background. I was pushed to become his papal representative. 'Pope John XXIII threw open the windows of the Vatican and your Polish Pope has gone and closed them again.' (This is a somewhat bowdlerised version of what Eddie actually said.) And even now not a conversation goes by where I am not held to account for my compatriot's apparently reactionary views although, in truth, I think he was the most radical of popes. I should not be surprised if his failures, such as they were, were not, to some degree, due to Eddie's example. Would Christendom survive, were it made to accommodate him? Anyway I have never once heard the editor of *Aquarius* speak of the author of *Evangelium Vitae* without a chain of expletives. I will not repeat here what the Holy Father had to say about Eddie.

Maurice Leitch

Ward's Irish House, London, 1971

Often, he had supped in this basement den, in the past, a place to catch up with those visiting writers and artists over to cadge a publisher's or a BBC cheque whilst keeping up a studied front of insolence and free-loading disdain towards their benefactors. The last time he had headed down these dark stairs a bristling duo of young Belfast poets on the literary up and up had ignored their editor to spend the entire afternoon challenging one another as to who possessed the more authentic 'Ulster voice'.

On this particular day, descending the stairs, he was met by the smell of bacon and boiled cabbage, and remembered the Thursday ritual of it being served to soak up the pints of stout already crowding the bar like so many dark, creamy-headed sentinels.

As expected, the place was full, the seating arranged in four strictly designated areas around the walls of the moss-green, Art Deco-tiled room, each with the name of a Province outlined above it in curling Hibernian script.

Crilly was waving to him from the Munster section, at his back the horse-shoe shaped booth holding a full complement of drinkers, thighs touching, in a kind of enforced huddle, and all with the air of men with a careful control of their bladders, anxious not to lose their place even if the moment arrived for them to go seeking the Gents.

"Over here!" came Crilly's breezy call, and as he made his way across the uneven, flagged floor he became conscious of eyes homing in on him from all four Provincial corners of the big room, the sheer concentrated intensity of that stare unsettling, so that by the time he reached the haven of Munster he was sweating freely.

"Come, take the weight of your legs," Crilly commanded, and one of the group, a tousle-haired, romantic looking youth in a heavy overcoat despite the heat, dutifully pressed himself up hard against the end of the booth, giving him a sideways, nervous grin as he did so.

Squeezing into the space provided he experienced a sudden rush of warmth towards the young guy, almost visualising that tattered, much submitted manuscript burning a hole in the inside pocket of his trailing old Crombie.

Once upon a time, not so long ago either, he, too, had been like that, same embarrassed smile, reacting too fast, too gratefully, to every quip and comment, no matter how banal or boring. But then some things, certain personal traits, never change. He felt like telling the young lad that, and if he'd had more drink on him almost certainly would have done, slipping into the role of this wiser, much older man who'd been around the block a few times.

Eamonn O' Doherty

Juggling Bishops, page 134
monotype

Enda McDonough

Guests of Creation

The phrase is George Steiner's. It came back as I reflected on Sean Hutton's summary of Eddie's life and work. I was last introduced to Eddie at The Patrick Kavanagh weekend in Inniskeen Co Monaghan in November 2004. I have never had the privilege of knowing him well, although I picked up copies of *Aquarius* when I could and I share some of Eddie's enthusiasms and causes from peace-promotion to poetry, as well as some of his convictions about 'little' magazines, and at least a whiff of his complex attitudes to the official Catholic Church.

As a theologian trying to make some sense, if that be possible, of the God-cosmos-humanity relationship, I have had to return again and again to the mysterious spheres of creator and creativity, creating and creation in subject, process and product. As I attempted my theological exercise, I turned again and again to explore human versions of the creation mystery from forming a sentence, a human relationship or a peaceful community to writing a poem and to the working of musicians, painters and sculptors. The sheer graciousness of all these activities, of their human agents and of their end products prompts the first responses of delight, reverence and gratitude. One indeed feels a privileged guest in the presence of such people and their gifts. It is after that fashion that I am sometimes enabled to grasp what the Book of Genesis and the other poetic, biblical accounts of divine Creator and (continuing) divine creation/creating are saying. It is along those lines that I interpret (perhaps mistakenly) Steiner's description of human beings as guests of (divine) Creation and of the (divine) Creator.

Eddie Linden played grateful guest in his employment of his own creative gifts as person and poet, and of gracious host as editor and party-giver. Made in the image of the Creator God, he remains a gift to us.

Wesley Murphy

Dear Eddie, are you really seventy?

You have been a presence in my life since I met you in Hampstead one early autumn morning in 1960. You were a red haired kilted Scot, a Van Gogh look alike, who in the last few years has metamorphosed into an Irish man. And in fact you are both: born among the thorny gorse of Co. Tyrone, but fostered and raised in the unforgiving streets of the Glasgow tenements. These paps of your 'City of Razors' made you the driven soul you are today.

Do you remember those Hampstead years of the early sixties, when we Scots and Irish writers, poets, folk singers and actors met for our bowls of potato soup in the Witches Cauldron, or drank dreadful English bitter and stale tea in our seedy bed sits? There were, of course, times when the Irish actress, Sally Travers, satisfied your hunger in her welcoming 'open house'. I seem to remember, Eddie, that for many months you slept on a mattress in her bathroom, sharing it with her cats.

And when you were struggling with your sexuality, burdened with guilt about your own preferences, you were on the receiving end of a beating outside the gay pub, The William IV, after haranguing the drinkers there, like a latter day Jeremiah, over the evil of their ways. Or, years later, another punch landed on your eye when you caught your local priest *in flagrante* with one of his female parishioners, the blow being delivered by the man of God himself

But, Eddie, in spite of many punishments and disappointments, you were always true to yourself. And your male friends, homo- and heterosexual, have always stood by you. Perhaps we were in awe of your absolute integrity in pursuit of your dream. Your female friends, too, have shown great loyalty. After Sally and Elizabeth, there have been Jennifer, Constance and Mary, surrogate mothers and affectionate supporters, sustaining you in your 'holy poverty' and always there to provide the itinerant poet with 'a wee crust'. The traumas you experience in the mid sixties had a happy outcome. You discovered poetry. From then on, the promotion of *Aquarius* became your life's passion. You helped so many 'wee poets' to get published that I believe, in the future, you will be seen as a kind of midwife to the poetic expression of the late twentieth century. Like a picaresque character from Defoe's London, you were inexhaustible in promoting your magazine.

Who else could have lived in a tiny bedsit in Maida Vale, sleeping on a mattress, with army blankets, the only other furniture piles of *Aquarius* magazines almost up to the ceiling? Who else would have been driven enough to flog your copies outside cinema queues and in pubs and then to cart a caseload of them across the Atlantic to Toronto, Ottawa and New York? Indeed, the battered suitcase you arrived with in Toronto weighed almost as much as your thin frame. Yet, you sold every copy and *Aquarius* survived.

Those who outlive you, Eddie, had better make sure that Westminster Cathedral will be the venue for your leave taking. Your coffin should be draped in the Red Flag, and you should be serenaded into the hereafter with the 'Internationale' and 'A Nation One Again.

May you live to be a hundred, and continue to be the scourge of bigotry and humbug, whether of the Orange, Green or Philistine variety.

With great affection…

'When I was sixteen...'

When I was 16 I worked in the poetry department at Better Books in Charing Cross Road. It was 1971. The shop was buzzing and writers such as Bob Cobbing, Bernard Kops and Seamus Heaney often dropped in. William Burroughs, droll, steely-eyed and ashen-faced, was a regular customer.
Eddie Linden walked in one day, clutching a half bottle of Scotch and a tatty shopping bag stuffed full of the first issue of *Aquarius*. I'd never met him before. Within minutes he had somehow persuaded me to take a dozen copies on sale or return. Every morning afterwards he came back to see if I had sold any.

Eddie and I struck up a friendship. I was rather shy then. He was not. He spoke his mind. When he dropped in to the shop he used to say the most outrageous things about the customers, especially if they were writers or publishers. When the late distinguished film critic Alexander Walker, a loyal customer who sported a huge bouffant hairdo, walked in, Eddie said loudly to me: 'Och, look at that wee poof! Have you seen the shite reviews he does?' A rep from a major publishing house was greeted with the words 'Ah pity anyone that ends up on your poetry list. It'd be the kiss of death!'

One day I told Eddie that my father was the Irish poet Patrick Galvin. 'Ah want to meet him,' said Eddie. 'Take me to him.' My father lived in Brighton then, so I took Eddie down one weekend by train. My father was very welcoming to Eddie. 'Let's have a talk,' he said. So Eddie talked about Irish poetry, history, drama, politics, religion and sex all night. At four in the morning my father was a wreck. Eddie was not.

At breakfast the next day my father, bleary-eyed and face heavily drawn, sipped black coffee in silence. Loudly Eddie said, 'Och, so what are your views on *Finnegan's Wake* then?' My father nearly choked. Eddie went on to talk about James Joyce until it was time for his train — which left at lunchtime.
On the journey back Eddie said how much he had enjoyed himself and then added: 'Do you think ah created a wee impression with your father?' Actually my father liked Eddie very much and he sent him a handful of new poems for *Aquarius*, one of which was 'The Mad Woman of Cork'. Eddie became a big champion of my father's work and always went to his poetry readings in London — often with a crowd in tow.

Friend and boon companion for over thirty years, Eddie always seems to me to be as outrageous as when I first met him. I bumped into him recently in the street and he suddenly dragged me round to poet Matthew Sweeney's flat. There he got up on a chair in the kitchen and started to loudly recite some of my Dad's poetry. 'Did you ever hear poetry read like this?' he said. No, she hadn't, said a less-than-amused Mrs Sweeney. Last week Eddie rang me, outraged, to tell me that a famous Catholic newspaper was being run by 'a band of homosexuals.' 'It's unbelievable!' he said.

My Dad lives in Cork now and since a recent stroke had been a bit incapacitated. But when I told him that Eddie was going to have a 70th birthday party he did a great take-off of him:
'Ah think he'll create a wee impression,' he said with a smile.

Glenn Patterson

'Skip forward fifteen years…'

Skip forward fifteen years. I am on a train with one hundred and five other writers, a roundabout trip from Lisbon to Berlin. Spain, France, Belgium, northern Germany, Poland, the Baltics, Russia, Russia, Russia, Belarus, Poland again and back over the Oder. Six weeks, eleven countries, three alcohol zones: wine, beer, endless versts of vodka. The bar is open more often than not. Even the soberest of us (and I am number eighty-something) have a hard job staying on the rails. 'Train of Drunks', screams a Moscow tabloid, over a picture of our Icelandic novelist ('they asked the other one first, but he was too busy to join the train'), high-stepping down the platform, past the welcoming band, the school children offering bread and salt, singing their song of happiness and peace.

The bar is more often open, but even when it's not the bar-car is a market for the exchange of books and journals and scraps of paper: ideas for collaborations; names of festivals, translators, funding bodies, still other books and journals. So it's no surprise when one day, resting my head on the window, I am reeled right back to this night a term into my big MA, I boarded the boat train in Euston, two unpublished stories under my belt, and a couple of tins in my rucksack to carry me through to Stranraer.

The boat train is a long drought for the unprepared. The boat train is a protracted pain in the neck for the passenger landed with a neighbour keen to talk.

The boat train is two minutes from departure and I have a space beside me (my theory has worked: always sit rear-facing, always wear a scowl; comfort at least to Rugby!) when I see you pass the window, walking like the bastards are right on your heels, and I know at once you are headed for me.

You are prepared for the drought. You are keen to talk.

You are, I think, as the train pulls out, so full of shit: Irish Embassy, Harold Pinter, Questions in the House, *Aquarius*, Adrian Mitchell…'Adrian Mitchell?' I say and think I've got you. 'I know his daughter.'

You say her name. You know her too.

On a boom-box behind us Bronski Beat plays. 'Alone on a platform the wind and the rain…' You turn in your seat.

'Wee Jimmy Somerville,' you say. You know him too.

You know 'City of Razors' by heart. Rugby has long been and gone. There is a gang of us now, talking back and forth; the carriage an anthology of anecdote. Eddieted.

There is early morning drinking on the boat across to Larne, then the long sobering walk from York Street station into town. You leave me with an *Aquarius* and an inkling to carry with me on the train back to the big MA. It's not about a living, but a life.

Robin Prising

Just an Ordinary Love-Letter

Was he flaxen-haired? Or a pale redhead? I couldn't tell as he lurked behind the shelves at Housman's Bookshop. Probably in the Summer of 1963. All at once I recognized his face from peace rallies at Trafalgar Square, from shoutings at Hyde Park Corner, from Aldermaston Marches. 'You're a pacifist, aren't you?' I asked, when he had finally cornered Willie Coakley and myself near the entrance.

'I'm a pacifist Communist anarchist Roman Catholic homosexual working-class Scot!' he replied in a single breath, neatly trilling all his Rs. 'Well, we're nearly everything of that, and Willie, if not a Scot, is a good Celt, an Irish one.' And with that quite said, Eddie Sean Linden became our fast friend for life.

Later, in some pub, we were talking about poetry. 'Did you know Dylan?' asked Eddie. 'Dylan Thomas, yes, I met him several times and admired his poetry and readings, but it's George Barker who interests me more.' 'But do you know John Heath-Stubbs?' Eddie asked. 'Only by name,' Willie said, 'the Blue-Fly poems!' Before we knew it we were off to the Catherine Wheel to meet the poet whom we now consider the King of the Cats. And for a decade there were hefty dinners with John Heath-Stubbs and Eddie at Schmidt's in Charlotte Street, now long-gone alas, which I had known since the ration-book years shortly after the War.

Eddie's interest in poetry was growing fast, leaping & bounding into an obsession. One began to worry about it. One began to worry about him. One thought he was ready to explode. The explosion came: it came in the form of *Aquarius* magazine, a real poetry magazine for real poets and real friends of poets and of poetry. And at the same time Eddie was finding his own voice in poetry.

Our Eddie is not a man who is merely out for Number One. He's out for Number Two and Number Two means You. Imagine my surprise opening a blue envelope with a note saying: 'Thought you'd like this. Love, Eddie' It was a fine review of my own book Manila, Goodbye, which had just appeared in the Sunday Times. With his generosity and ever-vigilant eye, Eddie sent it to me, by air, post-haste — my publishers would have taken nine months! And even though my book is in mere prose, Eddie, generously, had it reviewed in *Aquarius.*

In no time Eddie's Aquarius ranged about the poetry of the English-speaking world, honouring the best poets with special issues. Unlike the other magazines, which were locked up in the folk-pop idiom — a phoney brand of American English — *Aquarius* recognized that there was very much more than one poetry in English: Irish and Scots English, of course, Cornish and Welsh English, Australian and Canadian English, and the English of India. Yes, Eddie, you have made *Aquarius* cosmopolitan, and that poetic constellation of yours has risen even over the Antipodes. Eddie, I think of you always, I think of you wearing that kilt hitching rides on the roads to Spain; on your mad trips to Ireland, to Scotland, hunting down lost relatives; in your days at Oxford; as editor and publisher. I think of you flying over to New York on St Patrick's Day and Willie's meeting you as you crossed the St Patrick's Day Parade — to a car-bomb explosion! — while I by merest chance caught you both on television as you scurried, hand in hand, for cover. I think of you in all of our flats from Chesterfield Street to Vicarage Gate to Sloane Gardens, our dinners, by now at the Chelsea Kitchen, as we steered you away from pubs when you were forbidden drink (though not, perhaps, the Queen's Elm or the Queen's Head). And I think of all the friends you introduced us to, too many to mention by name, for Eddie you are a man of connexions and as willing to make friends as you are eager to share your friends. God bless you, you damned good 70-year-old (I'm 72) pacifist-Communist-anarchist-Roman Catholic-homosexual-working-class-Scot, Eddie Sean Linden, you — again like me — beloved bastard!

Trevor Royle

You'll have met Eddie Linden then?'

You'll have meet Eddie Linden then? The question came not so much as a polite enquiry but as a tart piece of inquisition from one of Scotland's best poets. Let's call him Norman MacCaig because he was the man asking the question and I kind of guessed that he was testing me to see how I would respond. The time was the mid-1970s and I was working for the Scottish Arts Council as its Literature Director, a job that required some delicate tightrope walking. In fact it was an easy question to answer. I had indeed met Eddie on one of my forays to London as a member of the council of the Poetry Society and he had left me in little doubt that *Aquarius* was on the agenda. Contrary to those who clearly did not know Eddie or had only come across him in full-on confrontation mode, we got on famously and he certainly gave the lie to an early piece of advice proffered by the same Norman MacCaig, a great man and a fine poet: 'Scottish writers are awfully fond of slapping each other on the back. Too bad they forget to remove the dirk first.'

Shortly before I left the Scottish Arts Council in 1979 we combined with the Greater London Arts Association to help produce a special edition of *Aquarius* dedicated to the memory of Hugh MacDiarmid who had died the previous year. Guest edited by Douglas Dunn, it contained many fine things, not least a luminous reminiscence by G. S. Fraser and a selection of short essays on 'What it feels like to be a Scottish poet'. Looking at it again, a quarter of a century later, it still holds good. Few would argue with a selection that included Stewart Conn, Duncan Glen, Kathleen Jamie, Liz Lochhead and Edwin Morgan, all of whom represented and continue to represent the best of writing from Scotland.

But it is not just the contents that marked *Aquarius*. It was and is a reflection of the man who founded it and edited it. Glancing through the pages of that distant edition of *Aquarius* is like looking into the world of Eddie Linden. Just look at the advertisers who cheerfully supported the venture, a litany of names that helped to people Eddie's life — from Martin Brian & O'Keeffe, by way of the Castle Lounge in Dublin, through the Cambridge Poetry Festival to Milo's Kebab House, not forgetting Jay Landesman, Bananas and the Poetry Review. Those were the signs in the territory and for those familiar with them they won't be easily erased.

Gerald Mangan

Linden after the fall
pen and ink drawing

Eddie (in search of a bed for the night): 'I'm homeless, Norman
MacCaig (conveniently deaf)
'I know you're hopeless, Eddie —
you don't have to tell ME.'

Clare Short

An Honourable Deception? (excerpt)
New Labour, Iraq, and the Misuse of Power

'To join the Privy Council we were gathered together in groups and trained to kneel on the first footstool and then move up to another and kiss the Queen's hand (not too firmly, or grasp her hand too hard) after we took our oath. I was among the first group of women to take the oath and we discussed how impossible it was for people like me to consider curtseying. But we were told the Queen was quite relaxed about this and we could show our respect, as we do to the Speaker in the Commons, by bowing our heads.

As the ceremonies were being organised, I suddenly knew I must ask for the Catholic oath. When I came to the Commons I had affirmed rather than take a religious oath, but as I took on this historic title, I thought of all my ancestors who had been persecuted for being Catholics. Near Crossmaglen, my Uncle Paddy, my father's youngest brother, has a few fields where he grazes cows and if you walk across them, you come to a Mass rock in a dip on the hillside where my ancestors used to attend Mass with watchouts posted in case the troops were coming to arrest them. I felt that I should represent all of them as I took my oath. Some of the rest of our group affirmed and others took the Anglican oath, but my ancestors and I inconvenienced them by requiring that the Catholic oath also be read out.

Once this was done, the Queen said a few cheerful and friendly words to each of us and then off we went to get on with our work.'

Tommy Smith

'Clad in kilt and tam o shanter'

'It was a Christmas week...'

It was Christmas week, a time of home coming and shopping, and Grogan's was no exception, crowded with shoppers, travellers, and regulars. Then the door opened, and in came Eddie, the man from God knows where. He was weighed down with his travel case and, of course, the regulation plastic bag. He edged his way through the throng at the bar, asking me to look after the travel case. Then, taking the recently published *Aquarius* from his plastic bag, he presented me with a copy duly signed by its editor. With a perplexed look on his face, he made a string of enquiries about mutual friends, asking where he could contact them. In the same conversation, he told me his travel arrangements — as usual, he was going to Constance Short for Christmas, and afterwards he was going to John Behan in Galway.
Eddie, an almost always Christmas visitor, is a great man to gather together old friends in the world of the arts. Like the Pied Piper, he relentlessly pursues them to their haunts. Among his literary and artist friends, he is very obviously happiest. His love of literary endeavour is easy to see when he is immersed in a good discussion on the merits of literature, or swapping stories of events in London and Glasgow, while at the same time absorbing tales of the Dublin scene. For me, Christmas would have a big void if Eddie did not make his journey.

Always the parting words, 'I will see you next Christmas' — and then a quietly spoken afterthought: he says to me, 'I am getting together another *Aquarius*; any chance of a wee ad?' Safe journey, Eddie, you are priceless.

Sydney Bernard Smyth

Wandering Poet Steps Ashore.

Eddie Linden breezed into the Inishbofin Arts Festival in 1977. (It blew a gale all week - several gales.) The "official" programme was already full - large sums having been raised on the promise of "a celebration of Bofin's numerous links with artists & writers," & used to deliver a list which ignored most of the links this writer, then in his seventh year of residence in that island, was aware of. The organising committee gave us "names." Some of them had no previous acquaintance with North Connemara, & took no trouble to talk to the locals. When this issue - what art had to do with the people - was addressed in my play *Don Bosco Grainne & the Dole* one visiting journalist* accused me of putting words into the islanders' mouths; which argument one of them forcefully rebutted: "he didn't make us say half enough!"
Anyway, at one day's notice, it fell to me to try to arrange a reading for Eddie. Because there was no time to advertise, I went round all my neighbours in the adjacent West Quarter, & an audience of more than a dozen turned up, among them Frank Halloran & Patsy Coyne - parents with sizeable families - & Martin McCann who had spent years at sea, & had worked on Clydeside, & knew something of the world - as indeed they all did; there was hardly a family or a bachelor in Bofin who had not had close personal experience of the greater industrial entity over the eastern horizon.

Eddie read at lunchtime in the bar in Murray's hotel, with a wide-window sea view of a scattering of islands to the south. The attendance was riveted. They understood immediately what this anguish was about. City of Razors made a startling impact. The directness of the language - what local usage described as the Bowery - so far from giving offence, enhanced the effect. This was no stranger they were confronted with.

There could not have been a greater contrast between Eddie Linden's grass-roots contact with the island people & the reading later in the week in the Inishbofin Parish Hall by Richard Murphy, who delivered his Cleggan Disaster epic - which reads very well on the privacy of the page but lives up to its title when delivered in public by its author, a decent man but one whose command of voice technique (lines like "high in the sky" pitched in the counter tenor's register, "low under the sea" in a mock-Chaliapin basso-profundo) is somewhat limited. *The Irish University Review* reported this event, with bland academic mendacity, thus: "there wasn't a dry eye in the house... Packed to the rafters with islanders..." In fact, Inishbofin people present numbered 78-year-old Pat Concannon, from whom Murphy got the story; his daughter & 3 grand-daughters; his two sons who crept in at the back ten minutes from the end, along with Michael Burke & John Cunnane. The remainder of the audience were some eighty tourists. After the obligatory photo-op with Murphy & committee members, Pat while being driven back to Murray's confided: "Poetry is very boring." The small crowd whom Eddie's earlier reading startled into what Mr Eliot referred to as another kind of reality, had no such reservations. They not infrequently spoke of him in years that followed.

*For more detail on this, see the novel FLANNERY (Odell & Adair, 1991).

Trevor Tolley

How I Got to Know Eddie Linden – And Why I Shouldn't Have

Life was easier back in 1983 — I had never heard of Eddie Linden. Then one day a parcel arrived. It contained copies of a periodical that was new to me, *Aquarius* – the Special Canadian issue — with a note that someone had told the sender (Eddie Linden) that I might be interested. Who that person was I have never been able to find out. There was no request for payment, so I didn't reply. That was where I started to go wrong. Not long afterwards another letter arrived, saying that no payment had been received. Complimentary copies that were followed by a request for payment were new to me — though perhaps not in Eddie's world. At any rate, because literature seemed a worthy cause, I sent Eddie some money. For all I knew, of course, he might just go out to a local hostelry; and, when funds got low, send a similar 'complimentary copy' to some other likely donor.

Some months later, it occurred to me that I might try to get my money's worth. Among Eddie's friends was John Heath-Stubbs, whom I knew as a respectable writer; and I felt that that might be some indication of a certain respectability concerning Eddie too. My book, *The Poetry of the Forties*, was due to come out shortly; and it seemed to me that there might be a possibility of enhancing its fortunes if I could touch Eddie for a special "Poetry of the Forties" issue of *Aquarius*. I met Eddie, and he agreed that my idea was a good one. What also seemed good to him, I sensed, was that I had a source of financial support for the project. My old friend Roy Fuller agreed to send me some unpublished poems from the forties; and, with this mark of approval, I was able to induce a number of writers from that lost decade to contribute. Here I encountered Eddie's special talent. He seemed to know everybody. There was nothing tentative or hesitant in his approach. We were walking along a street in Notting Hill Gate after visiting John Heath-Stubbs (duly lined up), when Eddie asked me if I had thought of approaching Gavin Ewart for something. I said I hadn't, because I didn't know him. We were passing a telephone box. Eddie hustled us both in, dialled a number, and then proceeded to tell Gavin that Professor Tolley was doing something on the poetry of the forties, and that I wanted to talk to him about it. So I talked to Gavin, who had no idea who I was, and (as I later discovered) did not know that it was an issue of *Aquarius* that I was talking about. But he agreed without any persuasion. That was Eddie's touch. Later he sent me a list of people whom he felt I should approach, even though I already had a good idea of whom I wanted. There followed other *urgent* letters, telling me that I mustn't omit to contact this one or that. The people seldom refused; but, in the end, I had to tell Eddie that I could only ask for contributions a few at a time: if everybody he suggested agreed to contribute, we would have an *Aquarius* as big as the telephone book.

The "Poetry of the Forties" special issue was a notable success; though the printer managed to produce about a quarter of the copies with randomly distributed blank pages, which gave rise to near nervous-breakdown in Eddie. I found myself in the irregular position of being a regular Guest Editor — at such times as funds became available (which was not too often). We had issues in honour of Roy Fuller, John Heath-Stubbs, and a double whammy on George Barker and W.S. Graham. Eddie's letters, suggesting writers to be approached, with long P.S.'s listing names he had forgotten to include in the main body of the letter, were a regular feature of being a Guest Editor. In these letters there would be cautions to avoid a certain poet; or not to forget another writer who would be offended if not asked to write about an old friend. As I had frequently not heard of some of the people concerned, I was a bit nervous about how to put my foot forward. But I did, and things turned out rather impressively.

At times I was called on to smooth things over when they went wrong. The cover of the Barker/Graham issue reproduced a picture by Craigie Aitchison. It didn't come out quite right. Eddie had another near nervous-breakdown. I agreed to call Craigie, who merely said that that sort of thing happened. I liked the picture, and foolishly asked how much it would cost. About forty thousand pounds, Craigie thought. That again was Eddie: he could get friends to let him use valuable pieces of art and literature for nothing.

Now we have an issue in honour of Eddie, who is about to be seventy, and everybody is again happy to contribute. I feel Eddie has made a fine achievement over the years with the many issues of *Aquarius*; and I salute Eddie with my very best wishes for many more of them — but no more of those letters.

Now I can shed the cross!
linocut

Constance Short

Richard Tyrrell

From South America

America traces the coming of age of three children – Esteban, Chichi and Kiki. In late adolescence, they have become 'children of the Convento'. They support their families by begging below the high walls of the Convento de la Popa. Act One follows the three through a morning below the walls. They amuse themselves by telling each other stories and playing games.

Scene: The Difference between Esteban and Kiki.

ESTEBAN: Is it true that your mother was a maid for Imelda Turriago?

KIKI: Where did you hear that?

ESTEBAN: It's part of our heritage of myths, rumour and gossip.

KIKI: No, she was never a maid. Imelda wanted her for a maid, because Imelda wants to have power over people she has no power over.

ESTEBAN: But she's powerful already.

KIKI: She has no power over my family.

CHICHI: When did she want your mother for a maid?

KIKI: Years ago, Imelda bought a house in Getsemani, with a courtyard and a tamarind tree. She put shutters on the window, and a walnut dresser with personitas by the wall, and a long chair, and a painting of a chiva. She wanted a maid to stay all day while she went to an office to bargain with bus drivers and factory hands.

CHICHI: What was she before she went into the tourist industry?

KIKI: She was my mother's friend in girlhood.

ESTEBAN: Ah, there's a story in this. Tell it, Kiki.

CHICHI: Talk, Kiki. Your turn.

KIKI: (Reluctantly.) All right … Imelda Turriago grew up in a house with a strange name. It was called, The House Where Girls Go To Bed Because They're Hungry. My mother lived in a house just as hungry but where girls didn't go to bed. But whether girls do it for money or love, they'll always have things in common. And my mother and Imelda had one thing in common — they had vision. If you're not hungry, even for five minutes, you'll see the world, and see the things in it that make it visionary. They loved to see the clean flag rise over the Castillo, or a boy washing the hull of a boat, or a gardener pulling weeds around a yellow zinnia, or the reflection of your face in the floor. So my mother and Imelda were always friends. Imelda lived by opening her legs, my mother by waiting late at the harbour. After customers left, and the fishermen took fish for their families, they gave the leftovers to my mother rather than throw them into the sea. Because, you see, she charmed them. At dawn, she went into the town selling fish from a bag. Later she got a stall outside the Capilla del Mar. When she met my father, they spent their honeymoon under the stall, with the smell of fish, and that was where I was conceived. Imelda was such a good friend that while my mother was pregnant, no one else was allowed to feel me kick inside, not even my father. But money corrupted Imelda. She married a powerful man who was a regular, and then noticed all the tourists who came to see the colonial buildings and the flag rising over the Castillo. So she bought buses to take the tourists from their hotels to the Castillo and the Convento, and soon offered to buy my mother's spot outside the Capilla del Mar because it was an ideal place to sell tickets. My mother wouldn't sell for years, and it grew into a point of contention.

Imelda nagged so much that finally she sold. My mother was always pregnant and sick, and worn down. That was when Imelda offered to take her as a maid. Mama turned her down flat. She wouldn't be a maid for a whore.

ESTEBAN: What did she die of?

KIKI: She died.

ESTEBAN: How, Kiki?

KIKI: Death is death. It has its own reasons.

ESTEBAN: But how, Kiki?

KIKI: Every day, when she was ill, my father shook her awake at dawn, afraid she'd be dead. We had no money. He was so afraid that he went to Imelda, but she told him she'd do nothing to help. And one day, my father shook her, and she was dead. That's all. People die. It's God's will.

Silence.

ESTEBAN: This is why you're a very serious person.

KIKI: I'm a happy person, out of respect for my mother and father.

ESTEBAN: Why respect mothers and fathers? Mine rarely respect each other. Why should I respect them more than they respect themselves?

KIKI: That's the difference between you and me.

Note: Eddie Linden has been a friend for fifteen years. On my first arrival in London he was one of the most supportive people I met. He has remained so. I'd like to celebrate his 70th by offering a short extract from a play I've just drafted. R.T.

Snapshots
from Eddie's 70th
birthday party.
Crypt of St. Etheldreda's
Church Ely Place,
Holborn London.

DANNIE ABSE was born in Cardiff. Poet. President of the Welsh Academy. He practised as a doctor from 1950 to 1982. *'New and Collected Poems'* (Hutchinson 2003) is a Special Commendation of the Poetry Book Society. His most recent prose is *'The Two Roads Taken'* (Enitharmon) (2003).

The late HELEN ADAM, who loved Eddie Linden's poetry, was born in Glasgow in 1909. She lived in the States from 1939 until her death in 1993. Her poetry is available in her *Selected Poems & Ballads* (New York, Helikon Press) and in the forthcoming *Edinburgh Book of Twentieth-century Scottish Poetry*.

DERMOT AHERN is Minister for Foreign Affairs in the Irish Government and United Nations Special Envoy on UN Reform. He is a member of the Fianna Fáil Parliamentary Party representing the constituency of Louth in Dáil Éireann.

CRAIGIE AITCHISON CBE.,RA, was born in 1926 in Scotland, and studied at the Slade School of Fine Art London from 1952 - 54. In 1954 he was one of 'Six Young Contemporaries' at Gimpel Fils; in 1955 he was awarded a British Council Scholarship to study in Italy. He now lives and works in London.

CHRISTOPHER ARKELL, born in 1953, first met Eddie 25 years ago. Publisher of *The London Magazine*, Publisher and Editor of *The London Miscellany* and Chairman of The Miscellany Foundation.

LELAND BARDWELL was born in India, of Irish parents, grew up in Leixlip, County Kildare and now lives in County Sligo. She has published collections of poetry, novels, stage plays and radio plays and a short story collection.

GEORGE BARKER (1913- 1991) born in Essex and educated at LCC school in Chelsea and Regent St. Polytechnic. Lived in Japan, United States, Italy and England. At age twenty published first book of poems, *Thirty Preliminary Poems* followed by *Poems (1935) (*Faber and Faber) and many subsequent books of poetry and prose.

JONATHAN BARKER was Librarian of the Arts Council Poetry Library in London and now works in the Literature Department of the British Council. He has edited the poems of W.H. Davies and Norman Cameron and has edited a Bibliography of Poetry from Britain and Ireland since 1970.

SEBASTIAN BARKER lives in London, his books of poetry include *Guarding the Border: Selected Poems* (Enitharmon, 1992), *The Dream of Intelligence* (Littlewood Arc, 1992), *The Hand in the Well* (Enitharmon, 1996), and *Damnatio Memoriae: Erased from Memory* (Enitharmon, 2004). Documentary novel *Who Is Eddie Linden* (Landesman 1979). Since 2002 has been editor of *The London Magazine.* In press; *The Matter of Europe* (Menard Press)and *The Erotics of God.*

MARGARET BECKER was born in Dublin. Studied at NCAD and has been a member of the Graphic Studio Dublin since 1972. Founder member of Leinster Print Studio 1998, also works in stained glass and has received many Commissions. Awards: 1st Prize, International Sacred Art Exhibition, Print Award at Listowel Writers Week Biennale. She has exhibited widely in Ireland and abroad.

JOHN BEHAN born in Dublin 1938 now lives in Galway, Sculptor and Artist, Studied in NCAD, Ealing Art College and Royal Academy School, Oslo. Founder of Project Arts Centre and the Dublin Art Foundry. Notable sculptures include "*Arrival*" in UN Plaza and *Wings of the World* in Shenzen, China. He is a member of Aosdána.

NESSA BEHAN is a Fine Art Graduate and works as an Art Facilitator.

OLIVER BERNARD born 1925 has two sons and two daughters. RAFVR 1943-47. Labouring jobs 1947-55. Goldsmiths College (BA) 1950-53. Advertising copywriter 1956-64. Teaching (English and Drama) 1964-82. Published (1960-2001*):* *Country Matters* (poems); *Rimbaud Collected Poems; Apollinaire Selected Poems: Poems* (1983); *Getting over it* (autobiography) 1992. *verse etc.* (Anvil) 2001

GORDON BOWKER taught at Goldsmiths' College until 1991. Since then he has written biographies of Malcolm Lowry (*Pursued by Furies*), Lawrence Durrell (*Through the Dark Labyrinth*) and George Orwell (*George Orwell*), and contributed articles and reviews to the *London Magazine, TLS, Independent*, and *Guardian.*

ALAN BROWNJOHN is the author of twelve books of poems, a new Collected Edition appears in 2006. *A Funny Old Year (2001)* is his most recent novel. He also has made versions of two classic dramas: Goethe's *Torquato Tasso* (National Theatre and Radio 3) and Corneille's Horace (Lyric) Hammersmith.

RICHARD BURNS Poet, born London 1943. Based in Cambridge where he founded the International Poetry Festival. Recent books include: *Avebury*, E-book edition, 2003. *For the Living* (Selected Longer Poems), 2004; *U vreme su?e* (*In a Time of Drought*, Serbian edition), 2004; *Crna Svetloba* (*Black Light*, Slovenian edition), 2005, *Mavro Fos* (ditto, Greek edition), 2005.

PAT BYRNE born in Enniscorthy, Co Wexford, and educated at University College, Cork, has been by turn a teacher, a journalist and a freelance writer. He has ambitions to become a published poet, and is at present preparing a selection of his work for publication. He lives in County Dublin with his wife Carol.

JAMES CAMPBELL was editor of the New Edinburgh Review between 1978-82. He now lives in London, where he works for the Times Literary Supplement. He is the author of a number of books, including *Paris Interzone* and *This Is the Beat Generation.*

TONY CARROLL is a Child Psychiatrist living in Galway. He is convinced that he learnt more of value for his profession in the pubs and parties of bohemian Dublin and London in the nineteen sixties than in any clinical setting. He has written mainly for professional journals. This is his first essay into editing.

MARY CAULFIELD, University Lecturer living in Dublin, where she is Vice-President of the United Arts Club and of The Shaw Society and Founder and Chairman of the Irish Byron Society. Formerly Committee member of The Australia/Ireland Bicentennial Conference and also of The Merriman Society which published the prize-winning *America and Ireland,* 1776 - 1996.

ELIZABETH CHAPMAN (GLACKIN) - eldest of James and Mary (Carroll) Glackin's family of seven daughters - Elizabeth, Teresa, Ella (deceased), Mary, Francis, Carole, Patricia and one son, Father Edward Glackin. PP. St. Columba's View Park, Glasgow.

WILLIAM LEO COAKLEY an Irish and an American citizen, has published his poems on both sides of the Atlantic in anthologies and magazines such as *Aquarius* and the *London Magazine.* As an editor, he prepared the first publication of Sean O' Casey's revolutionary early play *The Harvest Festival.*

PATRICK CONYNGHAM, born Ireland 1959. Poet, novelist and visual artist with numerous exhibitions. Recent new books ' *Everything strange*' and '*Another feather down the canyon*' published by Tuba Press. Currently working on a novel '*Between the Hills*'.

ROBERT CREELEY (1926-2005), born Arlington, Massachusetts. Poet, essayist, playwright, letter-writer; A graduate of Black Mountain College where he taught and edited *The Black Mountain Review* (1954-7).Chancellor of American Academy of Poets (1999); New York State Poet Laureate; He wrote over sixty books of poetry including *For Love Poems (1950-1960);Selected Poems (1945-90).*

SIR BERNARD CRICK was professor of political philosophy first at Sheffield and then Birkbeck College, London. Author of *In Defence of Politics* and *George Orwell: a life,* he founded the Orwell Prize for political writing. He retired to Edinburgh where he met Eddie Linden in a bar via Sebastian Barker. Here for the first time in print is the popular version of his inaugural lecture of forty years ago.

ANTHONY CRONIN born in Enniscorthy, Poet, Essayist, Novelist, Playwright and Critic, author of several books of verse: *RMS Titanic, The End of the Modern World, The Minotaur and Other Poems (1999)* and *Collected Poems (2004).* His biographies include *Samuel Beckett, The Last Modernist.* He was cultural and artistic adviser to former Taoiseach, Charles J. Haughey. In 2003 was elected a Saoi of Aosdána.

HILARY DAVIES born London of Anglo-Welsh parents, read French and German at Oxford and currently is Head of Languages at St. Paul's Girls' School. A Hawthornden Fellow, she won the prestigious Eric Gregory award for Young Poets and the Cheltenham/TLS poetry competition and for ten years co-edited the poetry magazine, ARGO. In 1992 guest-edited *Aquarius Women* (19/20).

GERALD DAWE has published six collections of poetry, including *The Morning Train* and *Lake Geneva.* He teaches at Trinity College Dublin. He published several poems with *Aquarius* in the 1980s.

JOHN F. DEANE founded The Dedalus Press where he was editor until end 2004. He is General Secretary of the European Academy of Poetry, Irish honorary member of the Norwegian Academy of Literature and is a member of Aosdána. His latest collection is "*Manhandling the Deity*"(Carcanet) and his next collection will be "*The Instruments of Art*".

DIARMUID DELARGY studied at the University of Ulster and completed his post-graduate studies at the Slade School of Art in London. He is a painter, sculptor and print-maker, and has exhibited extensively nationally and internationally. He was elected to Aosdána in 1999 and to the Royal Society of Painter/Printmakers, Bankside, London in 2005.

FERGUS DELARGY born in Belfast 1958, University of Ulster 1976 –80, BA (hons). 81-82 MA. PSI fellowship New York City 1987. Albuquerque New Mexico 1995-97; Galway, Ireland.1997-. Lectures at GMIT Galway 1998. Exhibited in Ireland, USA, Mexico and Holland. Collections: AIB Arts Council NI. Private collections USA, Ireland, Holland.

MICHAEL DONAGHY (1954-2004), Poet and Irish Traditional Musician, born in New York and studied at Fordham and University of Chicago (edited Chicago Review). Moved to London in 1985. Published : *Shibboleth(1988),Errata (1993) Conjure(2000).* His many awards include Geoffrey Faber and Cholmondeley Awards, and Whitbread and Forward Prizes. He married Maddy Paxman, one son, Ruairí. Mike threw a wonderful party for Eddie's 60th Birthday and was in discussion with Eddie about a book to celebrate his 70th Birthday, when he tragically died.

JULIE DUFFY aged 14, granddaughter of Eddie Linden's cousin, Teresa Gallacher who is a sister of Elizabeth Chapman (Glackin) q.v.

PAUL DURCAN was born in Dublin, 1944 of County Mayo parents. Poet. *Christmas Day (1966), Greetings to Our Friends in Brazil (1999), The Art of Life (2004).* Ireland Professor of Poetry 2004 – 2007. Lives in Dublin.

GEOFFREY ELBORN was born in 1950, and amongst his books are biographies of Edith Sitwell and Francis Stuart. He has contributed to *Aquarius*, The Tablet, The Listener, The Scotsman, and The Guardian, etc. and most recently to The Oxford Dictionary of National Biography. He is living in Orkney at present.

ELAINE FEINSTEIN is a prize-winning poet, novelist and biographer. She was made a Fellow of the Royal Society of Literature in 1980 and her work has been translated into many languages. Her widely praised books include biographies of Pushkin, Marina Tsvetayeva, Ted Hughes and Anna Akhmatova.

KATHERINE GALLAGHER is an Australian Poet resident in London since 1979. Her poems have been published widely in the UK and Australia. She has several collections, most recently *Tigers on the Silk Road* (Arc Publications, 2000)

PATRICK GALVIN Born in Cork in 1927, the author of seven collections of poetry, including *Folk Tales for the General* 1989, which was a Poetry Ireland Choice. His plays, including *The Last Burning*, have been regularly staged in Ireland and abroad. A member of Aosdána, his autobiography *Song for a Raggy Boy* was made into a film in 2003, starring Aidan Quinn.

SYLVIA GERAGHTY Solicitor of Supreme Court of Ireland; Solicitor of Supreme Court of England and Wales; A Lead Counsel at an International Criminal Tribunal (War Crimes).

ALWYN GILLESPIE studied Fine Art in Ulster College of Art and Design, and Art Teaching in National College of Art and Design. Has exhibited in Dublin where she runs "The Botanic Art School". Her illustrations have appeared in a number of publications.

ALASDAIR GRAY, born in 1934 and dwelling in Glasgow, became jack of several trades being unable to earn a living by one. He has written plays, novels, stories, verses, literary histories and political pamphlets; designed and illustrated books; painted portraits, landscapes, stage scenery and mural decorations. He cannot be taken seriously.

FIONA GREEN was born in India in 1943. Married Martin Green, publisher. She first met Eddie Linden in 1964 since when he has been a regular visitor to her Fitzrovia home in London.

MARTIN GREEN is a poet and author whose latest published collection is *A Night With Fiona Pitt-Kethley*. For many years he was a publisher, and among his authors was Hugh Mac Diarmuid, George Barker and Patrick Kavanagh, (whose poems he collected and published). For the past thirty years he has lived off and on in Cornwall.

GERRY HARRISON is a former film-maker, who in gracious middle-age has become a writer, having published *The Scattering*. He has combined this career with another in local politics, and is an extremely disillusioned Labour councillor in Camden. Now is relocating to Co. Clare, to run a bookshop in Ennis, where he will encourage writers and poets to give readings.

ANNE HAVERTY was born in Co. Tipperary and now lives in Dublin, Her first novel, *One Day as a Tiger*, won the Rooney Prize in 1997. Her poetry collection, *The Beauty of the Moon*, was published in 1999, and *The Far Side of a Kiss*, a novel, in 2000. She has worked as a journalist and scriptwriter and wrote a biography of Constance Markievicz. A novel *The Free And Easy* is due from Chatto in 2006.

DERMOT HEALY, born Westmeath in 1947 and now lives in Co. Sligo. Poet, playwright, author, editor, screen-writer (Our Boys). A poetry collection *The Ballyconnell Colours* was published in 1992. His novels include *Fighting with Shadows (1984); A Goat's Song (1994)* and *The Bend for Home (1996)*.He is a member of Aosdána.

SEAMUS HEANEY'S first volume of poems *Death of a Naturalist* appeared in 1966 and since then he has continued to publish poetry, criticism and translations. In 1972 he moved with his family from Belfast to Co. Wicklow. He now lives in Dublin and spends occasional short periods as poet-in-residence at Harvard.

JOHN HEATH-STUBBS born 1918, 'out of Staffordshire.' Poet, whose first volume of poetry appeared in 1942, since when he has been at the centre of English letters. He was awarded the Queen's Gold Medal for Poetry and an O.B.E. His autobiography, *Hindsights,* appeared in 1993. *Aquarius* 23/24 dedicated to him appeared on his eightieth birthday.

JOY HENDRY born Perth, Scotland 1953 but lived adult life in the wonderful environs of Edinburgh. Poet, playwright, and editor of *Chapman,* Scotland's Quality Literary Magazine since 1971. Doctor of Letters (Edinburgh University). Friends with Eddie since an explosive encounter at the first Cambridge Poetry Festival (1975).

JOHN HOGAN is a business man and writer who has recently retired from the commercial rat race. He has published poems, essays and reviews but feels that he has never devoted enough time to writing. He lives in County Galway where he is now exploring the possibilities of leisure.

CON HOWARD was a career diplomat. Consul General in Boston, Press Counsellor in The Irish Embassies in Washington and London and secretary of the Irish delegation to Council of Europe in Strasbourg and Paris. He is founder of Cumann Merriman, British Irish Association, the Society of St. Brendan and The Irish-Australian Conference for the Australian Centennial. He is vice-president of the United Arts Club.

JOHN HUGHES born in Belfast 1962. He has published four collections of poetry, the most recent being *Fast Forward* (Lagan Press) 2003. Lives in County Donegal with his familly.

PEARSE HUTCHINSON born in Glasgow in 1927 of Irish parents, reared in Dublin.The Dolmen Press published his first collections, *Tongue without Hands,* (1963) and *Expansions* (1969). Publications by The Gallery Press include: *Watching the Morning Grow* (1972), *Collected Poems* (2002) and *Done Into English* (2003); and *Faoıstın Bhacach (1969); Le Cead na Gréıne (1990*). He lives in Dublin where he co-edits *Cyphers.* Guest-editor of *Aquarius* 4 (Irish Edition) 1971. He is a member of Aosdána.

SEAN HUTTON born Dublin, 1940; educated UCD, Hull University; living in England since 1960s; author of four collections of poetry in Irish language; Honorary Secretary, Irish Texts Society since 1992; Chair, British Association for Irish Studies 1994-2002, has worked in education and voluntary sector development; community policy officer, Federation of Irish Societies.

ALAN JENKIN'S books of poems include *Harm* (1994), *The Drift* (2000) and *A Shorter Life,* (2005). For almost as long as he can remember he has been grateful to Eddie Linden for his friendship, encouragement and advice, and for the remarkable survival of *Aquarius.*

JUDITH KAZANTZIS is a poet, novelist and printmaker in Lewes, Sussex. Her last collection *Just After Midnight* (Enitharmon 2004) includes many poems for her parents Lord and Lady Longford who knew and admired Eddie. *Odysseus Speaking* under the title *No One Speaking* is from her collection *The Odysseus Poems: Fiction on the Odyssey of Homer* Cargo Press 1999.

JAMES KELMAN lives in Glasgow. He writes short stories, novels and plays, and the occasional essay.

BRENDAN KENNELLY has published poetry, novels, plays and critical essays. He is a member of the school of English, Trinity College, Dublin 2.

BRUCE KENT is Vice-President of CND and of Pax Christi.

BENEDICT KIELY was born near Dromore, Co. Tyrone in 1919, and attended University College Dublin. He has worked as a journalist, broadcaster and University lecturer in Ireland and in the USA. A renowned story-teller, he is the author of many novels, short story collections and other works of non-fiction. *Collected Stories* appeared in 2001.

MARIUS KOCIEJOWSKI poet, essayist, and travel writer, lives in London. He has published three collections of poetry, *Coast* (Greville Press), *Doctor Honoris Causa*, and *Music's Bride* (both Anvil Press). Most recently, he published *The Street Philosopher and the Holy Fool: A Syrian Journey* (Sutton Publishing, 2004).

ERNEST LAVERY was born in Belfast. He has had a versatile work career including Textile samplemaker, Bicycle wheelwright, Gold-miner, Freight Porter, Night manager of Café and Pinball Gallery and Language teacher, Co-wrote a play for Radio Eireann. Currently co-writing script for a feature film in animation.

MAURICE LEITCH was born in County Antrim and educated in Belfast. His first novel, *The Liberty Lad,* was published in 1965, followed by *Poor Lazarus,* winner of the 1969 Guardian Fiction Prize. *Silver's City* won the Whitbread Prize for Fiction in 1981. He has also written radio plays, short stories, and television screenplays and documentaries.

TOM LEONARD, Poet. His publications include *Intimate Voices, Access to the Silence* (both Etruscan Books, Devon) and *Collected Poems 1965-2004*. He teaches Creative Writing, part-time, at Glasgow University.

JAMES LIDDY lives in Milwaukee (founded by an agent of Jacob Astor) where he drinks in the Co. Clare pub and nightly visits the memory farmhouses of his grandparents in Cranny and Scariff. He tells his students on Astor Street of David Astor's response, "I think we're in furs." when asked what he was in, but they don't get it.

MICHAEL LONGLEY born in Belfast, studied Classics in Dublin University. He was Director of Combined Art at the Arts Council of Northern Ireland. He has published autobiographical prose and a number of books of poetry, the most recent being *Snow Water* (Cape). *Gorse Fires* (Secker) won the Whitbread Prize and *The Ghost Orchard* (Cape) was a Poetry Society Book Choice. He is a member of Aosdána.

JOHN LUCAS is Professor Emeritus of English at the universities of Loughborough and Nottingham Trent. He is the author of numerous scholarly and critical works and of seven collections of poetry, most recently *The Long and Short of it* 2004. Since 1994 he has been the publisher of Shoestring Press.

PADRAIC MacCANA born Tyrone 1943, was educated in Belfast and London (Birbeck). Taught for some years. Played club and County Gaelic football in the 60s. Won open Poetry Competition Listowel 1975. Poems in Irish Times, Irish Press, Sunday Tribune etc. Currently completing a verse play on the Flight of the Earls 1607.

ENDA Mc DONAGH is Professor Emeritus of Moral Theology at Maynooth University and Chair of the Governing Body of Cork University. He has lectured widely and published many books and articles. His latest book is '*Vulnerable to the Holy; In Faith, Morality and the Arts*', Dublin.

COLIN McGOOKIN born in Belfast where he lives. An active exhibiting artist and workshop facilitator, he undertakes projects as diverse as willow sculpture and mural programmes to animation and documentary films. An elected associate member of the Royal Ulster Academy.

ROGER McGOUGH born in Liverpool has published many books of poetry for both children and adults. Awarded the CBE in 2004 for services to literature, he lives in south-west London with Hilary and two of his four children. His autobiography *Said and Done* was published autumn of 2005.

BRIGHID Mc LAUGHLIN born in Dublin, where she now lives. She is a journalist, illustrator, stonecarver,writer of children's books and boxing-correspondent for Punch Magazine.

AONGHAS DUBH MACNEACAIL, born Isle of Skye 1942. Writes poetry and songs in both Gaelic and English. Two poetry collections in Gaelic and one in English. Translates and travels. Scottish Writer of the Year in 1997. Glad Eddie exists, otherwise he'd have had to be invented.

ALICE MAHER was born in Tipperary in 1956. She studied fine art in the late eighties at Cork and Belfast and was a Fulbright scholar at the San Francisco Art Institute in 1987. She represented Ireland in the 22nd Sao Paolo Biennale and has exhibited in Dublin, Paris, New York and London. Maher's work often takes the form of installation and can include drawing, sculpture, print and photography.

DEREK MAHON was born in Belfast in 1941, studied in Trinity College, Dublin and The Sorbonne. He is a member of Aosdána, has received the Irish Academy of Letters Award and the Scott Moncrieff translation prize. Gallery Press published *Collected Poems*, 1999 and *Harbour Lights*, 2006.

GERALD MANGAN is a Glasgow-born poet, journalist, playwright and illustrator, living in Paris. His collections include *Waiting for the Storm*. He is a contributor to the Times Literary Supplement, Poetry Review and Le Monde.

GERDA MAYER was born in Czechoslovakia in 1927 and came to England at the age of eleven. She has published several poetry collections, one of which was a Poetry Book Society Recommendation. In print are *Bernini's Cat* , and *Prague Winter* (autobiographical vignettes).

JOHN MINIHAN born in Dublin 1946, spent thirty-five years as Photo-journalist with the London Evening Standard and Daily Mail. Work exhibited in National Portrait Gallery London, I987; Centre Pompidou, 1986; retrospective at National Photographic Archive, Dublin 2000. Published 4 Books of Photographs. In 2006 he will have a number of exhibitions and a publication of Samuel Beckett Centenary Shadows (Hale, UK.)

JOHN MONTAGUE poet and fiction writer, was born in New York in 1929 and reared in Co.Tyrone by two aunts. He attended UCD and Yale University. His works include *Death of a Chieftain* (1964), *The Rough Field* (1972), *The Dead Kingdom* (1984), *Collected Poems* (1995). In 1998 he was appointed as first holder of the Ireland Chair of Poetry.

MARY MONTAGUE Dubliner: knows Eddie since late sixties at Poetry Society. Lives near him and over the years more a Martha than a Mary in his life. Now in honour of his biblical span a "one-poem banfile!"

JOHN MORAN born 1949 in South London. Documentary Photographer and Researcher. Took up photography seriously in 1974 with the help of a good friend, Red Daniels, a well known photographer and contributor to *Private Eye*. "Since then I have photographed the great and not so great. Among the greats one stands out: the one and only Eddie Linden, a good mate and a man I always enjoy meeting."

BLAKE MORRISON was born in Skipton, Yorkshire. His books include *The Ballad of the Yorkshire Ripper, When Did You Last See Your Father?, As If, Too True* and *Things My Mother Never Told Me.* he is currently Professor of Creative Writing at Goldsmiths College, London.

ANDREW MOTION born in 1952. He is Professor of Creative Writing at Royal Holloway College, University of London and was appointed Poet Laureate 1999. His most recent collection of poems is *Public Property* (Faber, 2002).

PAUL MULDOON born Co. Armagh in 1951, graduate of Queen's University, Belfast, Professor of Poetry at the University of Oxford, 1999 to 2004. Currently is Professor at Princeton University. Amongst his collections are *Why Brownlee left (1980); Quoof (1983); Meeting the British(1987); Madoc: A Mystery (1990); The Annals of Chile (1994); Hay (1998); Poems 1968 – 1998 (2001), and Moy Sand and Gravel (2002).*

WESLEY MURPHY is an actor and broadcaster. Belfast born, he has acted in Theatre, Television, Film and Radio, in England, Ireland, Canada and the U.S.A. His radio documentaries for the B.B.C. include *The Drennan Letters* and *Dufferin, The Eminent Victorian.*

PATRICK NEWLEY showbiz writer, He is a long-standing contributor to The Times and The Stage newspapers. He was press agent to the writers Robin Maugham and Quentin Crisp and he also acted as a manager for Douglas Byng and Mrs Shufflewick (Rex Jameson).

EILEAN NI CHUILLEANAIN born 1942 in Cork, and educated at U.C.C. and at Oxford; Dean of Faculty of Arts (Letters) at Trinity College Dublin. Co-editor of *Cyphers.* Her latest books of poetry are: *The Water Horse* with Medbh McGuckian, and from the Irish of Nuala Ní Dhomhnaill, Gallery Press, 1999 and *The Girl who married the Reindeer,* Gallery Press, 2001, Wake Forest 2002.

EAMON O'DOHERTY took a degree in architecture at U.C.D is also a painter, printmaker and photographer. He is best known for his large-scale sculptures, more than thirty of which are in public locations in Ireland, England, and the U.S.A. An award-winning artist, and for many years a Senior Lecturer in the Dublin Institute of Technology, he forsook academic life in 2002 to concentrate on artwork in his Wexford studio.

DESMOND O'GRADY born in Limerick 1935 has lived in Paris, Rome, USA, Egypt and now in Kinsale, Co.Cork. He has published many collections of poetry, translations and prose memoirs. Recent and forthcoming books include *On My Way* (Daedalus), *Kurdish Poems of Love and Liberty* (London), *My Alexandria* Bibliotheca Alexandria. He is a member of Aosdána.

BRIAN PATTEN'S collections of poetry include *Love Poems*, and *Armada* (Flamingo Books, HarperCollins) and the novel *Mr. Moon's Last Case* (Mystery Writers of America Award). He was awarded the Freedom of the City of Liverpool in 2001, and an honorary degree from John Moore's University in 2002 and won a Cholmondeley Award for Poetry. He is Fellow of the Royal Society of Literature. His latest book, *The Story Giant,* is an interweaving of World Fables.

GLENN PATTERSON was born in Belfast where he lives. He is the author of six novels: *Burning Your Own; Fat Lad; Black Night at Big Thunder Mountain; The International; Number 5; That Which Was,* A new novel, *The Third Party,* will be published in 2006.

TOM PAULIN was born in Leeds in 1949. He moved with his family to Belfast in 1953. After school in Belfast he attended Hull University and then Oxford University. He taught at the University of Nottingham from 1972-1994, and is now the G.M. Young Lecturer at Hertford College, Oxford. His most recent book is *The Road to Inver: Translations, Versions, Imitations* 1975-2003.

PETER PORTER born in Brisbane 1929, arrived in London in 1951 where he still lives and "is therefore among the most elderly poets working in the UK." Has had two-volume *Collected Poems*, 1961-1999, published by OUP and *Max is Missing* and *Afterburner* published by Picador. "Wishes Eddie long life and continued literary triumphs."

ROBIN PRISING, a resident alien in New York, is the author of *Manila, Goodbye* (U.S.: Houghton Mifflin; Britain: Heinemann and Corgi). It won the Christopher Award for representing 'the highest values of the human spirit.' An ex-civilian-POW in WW II, he has also been on the executive board of the War Resisters' League.

GABRIEL ROSENSTOCK is a poet, translator, haikuist and editor. His *Selected Poems* is due from Cló Iar-Chonnachta. Neo-bhakti poems appear on his website.

TREVOR ROYLE'S latest book is *Civil War: The Wars of the Three Kingdoms* 1638-1660, published by Abacus.

ANTHONY RUDOLF writes literary criticism, autobiography, fiction and poetry. He translates French, Russian and other poetry. He runs Menard Press and is an occasional lecturer and broadcaster.

BERNARD SAINT poet, is a Jungian member of The Group Analytical Society, and Council on Addiction. He sees patients through the National Drug Strategy.

DERMOT SEYMOUR was born in Belfast in 1956 and studied at University of Ulster. Was awarded P.S.I. fellowship to New York in 1987 and has received many bursaries from Arts Council of N Ireland and An Chomhairle Ealaíon. He has exhibited all over Ireland, UK, USA, Canada, Poland, Germany, Finland and France and is represented by Kevin Kavanagh Gallery Dublin. He is a member of Aosdána.

THE RIGHT HON. CLARE SHORT MP entered Parliament in 1983 as the member for Birmingham Ladywell. She served as Secretary of State for International Development from 1997 until her resignation from the Cabinet over the war in Iraq in 2003. *An Honourable Deception?* was published by Free Press in 2004. She lives in Birmingham and London.

CONSTANCE SHORT was born in 1944. Trained as a commercial artist, she has exhibited extensively and now prefers to make Art in Public places, inviting the public to participate, especially in mono-printmaking using text. She wrote: "Every breath I take is a political gesture" which she wants on her gravestone.

ELIZABETH SMART(1913-1986). *By Grand Central Station I Sat Down & Wept* (1945, 1966); *The Assumption of the Rogues & Rascals* (1978); *Collected Poems*, (1992). As well as supporting Eddie Linden and small magazines, notably *Aquarius*, she was troubled by the difficulty of explaining to a sceptic what art is, especially the art of poetry. What is 'the flash that's poetry?' 'It's the passion one word has for another.' This insight, that poetry is not a personal thing, but attraction between words in a language, creating 'shape' and 'order' for 'the amorphous pain', is found in her poem, *'What Is Art? Said Doubting Tim'*

TOMMY SMITH, was born in Co. Cavan, where he was reared on a farm. Aged 15 came to Dublin and worked McCauley's and Killane's licensed premises, but found a spiritual home in McDaids. Since taking over Grogan's he has continued the tradition of welcoming and supporting writers and artists and makes the occasional foray in that direction himself.

DAMIAN SMYTH was born in Downpatrick in 1962. *Downpatrick Races* (Lagan Press), appeared in 2000. A stage play, *Soldiers of the Queen*, played the Belfast Festival at Queen's in 2002 and was published in 2003. His second collection is *The Down Recorder* (Lagan Press, 2004). He is Literature Officer with the Arts Council of Northern Ireland.

SYDNEY BERNARD SMYTH, born 1936 in Glasgow, grew up in Portstewart, married Cindy Hoxie, flourished in Inishbofin, four children. Stage work includes *How to roast a Strasbourg Goose* - about political corruption & torture; an Abbey dramaturg thought such material called for 'rather more tact.' Latest publication *The immodest Proposal* 2005 (Lapwing).

RALPH STEADMAN born 1936 Wallasey, Cheshire. Author and Illustrator of books for children and adults. Theatre Designer. Writer of Opera Libretti .Writer for TV, newspapers and magazines. His works have appeared in many exhibitions and won many awards. Hon D.Litt. at University of Kent. Lives in Kent.

MATTHEW SWEENEY born Co Donegal, Ireland. Lived for many years in London. Now resident in Berlin. Published a number of books of poetry, most recently *Sanctuary* (Cape, 2004), and *Selected Poems* (Cape, 2002),. Also co-author of *Writing Poetry* (Hodder, 1997 – updated 2003), and editor, or co-editor, of several anthologies.

ANNE TALVAZ born in 1963 in Brussels and currently lives in China. A professional translator, she has translated works by many French, English and Spanish-language poets including John Ashbery and Jacques Dupin. Her own collections include *Le rouge-gorge américain* (La Main Courante, 1997). and *Imagines* (Farrago, 2001).

ANTHONY THWAITE born in 1930, has known Eddie for more years than he can remember. They agree about a few things (e.g. George Barker) but disagree about many more.

TREVOR TOLLEY is Professor Emeritus of Comparative Literary Studies at Carleton University in Ottawa, Canada. His books include *The Poetry of the Thirties* and *The Poetry of the Forties*. He was guest-editor of *Aquarius* 17/18, a 'Poetry of the Forties' special edition; *Aquarius* 21/22, the Roy Fuller special edition, *Aquarius* 23/24 the John Heath-Stubbs 80th Birthday edition and *Aquarius* 25/26 devoted to George Barker and W. S. Graham.

SHAUN TRAYNOR lives in London. Poet and Novelist, Editor of *Poolbeg Book of Irish Poetry for Children.*

RICHARD TYRRELL is senior editor with the Going-there group of websites. In the 1990s, he was a freelance writer for The Independent, Guardian, Sunday Times, and many British and overseas publications. He was chairman of the Poetry Society in England 1993/4 and contributing editor to the *Encarta Book of Quotations.*

CHARLIE WALSH born in Navan in 1939. Having been led astray at University, he came on a temporary visit to England in 1960 but has lived there ever since. He has published two books of poetry. Eddie has been a family friend since the late sixties when they were part of the Bloomsbury set, centred around publishers Martin Brian and O'Keeffe.

JOSEPH WOODS is a poet and Director of *Poetry Ireland.* His second collection *Bearings* was published by Worple Press in April 2005. He is a former winner of the Patrick Kavanagh Award.

MACDARA WOODS born Dublin 1942. 14 books, most recent, from Dedalus, *Knowledge In The Blood: New and Selected Poems*, 2000, and *The Nightingale Water* 2001, also several CDs most recent, *In The Ranelagh Gardens,* with composer Benjamin Dwyer, March 2005. New collection due in Spring 2006. A member of Aosdána.

1969	Aquarius 1, pp 44	Editor/Publisher: Eddie S. Linden Advisory Editors: John Heath-Stubbs, Alan Smith, Gordon Heard, John Ezard, Cathy Tether. Cover: Anna Mieke Lumsden.
1970	Aquarius 2, pp.40	Editor/Publisher: Eddie S. Linden. Advisory Editors: John Heath-Stubbs, Alan Smith, Gordon Heard, John Ezard, Cathy Tether. Cover: Anna Mieke Lumsden.
1970	Aquarius 3, pp. 73	Editor/Publisher: Eddie S. Linden. Advisory Editors: John Heath-Stubbs, Alan Smith, Gordon Heard, John Ezard. Cathy Tether. Cover: Crispin Rose Innes.
1971	Aquarius 4, pp. 82	Irish number, guest-edited by Pearse Hutchinson. Cover: Eamonn O'Doherty, Drawing by Kevin O'Byrne.
1973	Aquarius 6, pp. 137	Scottish issue, guest-edited by Tom Buchan. 1st grant-sub sidised issue: Scottish Arts Council. Cover: Crispin Rose Innes.
1974	Aquarius 7, pp. 109	Edited: Eddie S. Linden. Advisory editors: John Heath-Stubbs, Alan Smith, Gordon Heard, John Ezard, Cathy Tether. Cover: Chinese paper-cut provided by Fiona Green. Grant-support; Greater London Arts Association.
n.d.	Aquarius 8, pp. 117	Welsh issue, guest-edited by John Ormond Cover: George Barker. Grant support from Welsh Arts Council and Greater London Arts Association.
1977	Aquarius 9, pp. 77	Dedicated to the Memory of Colin MacInnes edited by Eddie Linden; Assistant editor John Heath-Stubbs. Cover: John Behan. Grant Support from Greater London Arts Association.
1978	Aquarius 10, pp.137	In Honour of John Heath-Stubbs, guest-edited by Sebastian Barker. Cover: Portrait drawing by Phillip Rawson. Portrait drawing by Gerry Mangan, three photographs by Chris Barker. Grant support from the Arts Council of Great Britain.
1979	Aquarius 11, pp. 126	In Honour of Hugh MacDiarmid, guest-edited by Douglas Dunn. Cover: Ian Cameron. Grant Assistance from the Scottish Arts Council and the Greater London Arts Association.

Compiled by Seán Hutton

1980	Aquarius 12, pp. 136	A general issue including poetry from Ireland, guest-edited by Jon Gulliver. Grant Support from the Northern Ireland Arts Council, the Greater London Arts Association and the Irish Department of External Affairs.
1981/2	Aquarius 13/14 pp.157	Canadian issue including general section, guest-edited by Katherine Govier. Cover: Ralph Steadman. Grant support from The Canada Council (Conseil des Arts du Canada) and the Greater London Arts Association.
1984/85	Aquarius 15/16 pp.136	A special Australian edition, plus new Irish poetry & general section, guest-edited by Mark O'Connor. Cover: Adrian Henri. Grant support from the Arts Council of Australia, the Northern Ireland Arts Council, the Greater London Arts Association, the Irish Arts Council and the Irish Department of External Affairs. Thirty-eight adverts.
1986/7	Aquarius 17/18 pp.148	A special 'Poetry of the Forties' edition, plus a general section, guest-edited by A.T. Tolley. Cover by Colin McGookin. Grant support from the Arts Faculty Research and Publications Fund of Carleton University, Ottawa, Canada, and the Greater London Arts Association.
1992	Aquarius 19/20 pp.135	Aquarius Women, guest-edited by Hilary Davies. Cover by Constance Short. Grant support from the Arts Council of England and the Paul Hamlyn Foundation.
1993	Aquarius 21/22 pp.124	Roy Fuller – a tribute, guest-edited by A.T. Tolley. Cover drawing by Ged Melling.
1998	Aquarius 23/24 pp.112	John Heath-Stubbs: 80th Birthday Issue, guest-edited by A.T. Tolley. Cover drawing by Hammond Journeaux. Two photo graphs by John Minihan and a drawing by Milein (Cosman) Keller. Grant support from the Arts Council of England.
2002	Aquarius 25/26 pp.186	George Barker; W.S. Graham, guest-edited by A.T. Tolley. Cover by Craigie Aitchison. Photos by John Minihan and Christopher Barker. Funding: London Arts Board.

Eddie with John Heath-Stubbs
(circa 1992) Photograph

Fiona Green

Personal Magic as Proto-Science

Epilogue

Tony Carroll

first slide

In the nineteen sixties and seventies the pioneer family Therapist, Virginia Satir achieved such amazing results with entrenched dysfunctional families that she was viewed as magical. Her clients invariably reported that they felt totally understood and that her advice was *spot-on*. Indeed so imperceptive were her interventions in some cases that those whose lives had changed radically did not attribute this to her. Dr. Satir outlined and demonstrated her approach in many workshops, but no-one could replicate her successes. Then Richard Bandler and John Grinder, one a gestalt therapist and the other a linguistics scientist, carefully studied her method and came to see that, in fact, her own account of her practice did not accord with her actual work. Their analysis revealed that Satir adopted a variety of communication styles and intuitively cued into each individual's dominant communication channel. In those whose main channel was visual, she would use visual language such as, "it looks like"; "The way I see it"; "the picture that's emerging is" and for the kinaesthetic, whom she would physically touch, placing a hand on their shoulder etc. she used phrases such as: " How does it strike you?" and "I have a gut feeling that…"; and likewise with those who had auditory dominance. This led Bandler and Grinder to write a number of books, in one of which, '*The Structure of Magic*' they described her startling new method, now termed Neuro-Linguistic Programming. Virginia Satir was dismayed when her actual method was explained to her, which she then considered as manipulative and ethically questionable. She required quite a deal of persuasion before continuing with her work.

next slide please

The 2003 Reith Lectures were delivered by the eminent neuroscientist Professor Vilayanur Ramachandran and published in a book entitled *The Emerging Mind*. In Chapter 3, called *The Artful brain*, proposing a new discipline, Neuro-aesthetics, Ramachandran lists ten universal laws of art. In the first of these laws, 'Peak Shift', with evidence from the ethological studies of Niko Tinbergen and with reference to the Chola bronze statue of Parvati, Ramachandran concludes: "In other words human artists through trial and error, through intuition, through genius, have discovered the figural primitives of our perceptual grammar. They are tapping into these...and what emerges is a Henry Moore or a Picasso."

next slide please

In the *Lamb* pub in Lamb's Conduit Street, London on a Saturday afternoon in 1969, whilst a poetry reading was in session upstairs, Rachel and I found ourselves talking to a sandy-haired man with a Glasgow accent, who informed us that he was Irish. Though never having heard of Eddie before, in a strange way I had a sense that I sort of knew him well, which I certainly came to do over the next couple of years. In March of 2005, Eddie telephoned and in a round-about way told me that his seventieth Birthday Party was being held not on its actual day, May 5th, but on June 2nd to avoid a clash with the General Election. Whether he feared that his birthday celebration would eclipse the election itself or affect the result, I know not. However the interests of democracy presumably were served. We chatted on, discussing the events at our last meeting, which had been at the Kavanagh Centenary Festival in Inniskeen on the previous November. There he had been with Constance Short of whom he now spoke with enthusiasm. Next I heard from Constance and of her relief that I was helping with the project as it had become bigger than she had expected; she would meet me in Galway at the weekend, which she did. The point I am making is that at no stage did I undertake to be a co-editor, I had not been asked, there had been no mention of it whatsoever, nor indeed of any intended publication. I can't say that there was misrepresentation as in fact there was no representation at all. Yet within two weeks of Eddie's phone-call, my house was filling up with manuscripts, I had three programmes running on the computer and there were back-up discs and documents scattered about the floor.

Over a span of thirty years Eddie produced seventeen issues of Aquarius and has acquired an enormous number of friends and well-wishers amongst artists, writers and arts administrators. They have responded most generously to our requests for contributions. An amazing achievement. How has he done it? For me becoming an editor and publisher of *Eddie's Own Aquarius* has been taxing and time-consuming and I had to learn a lot very rapidly. To my surprise I found that I enjoyed every minute of it. But how come Eddie identified me for the task. How did he know that I could do it and would do it?. Did he know me better than I knew myself? This is unsettling; after all I am supposed to be the psychiatrist. I console myself by believing that he does it intuitively. He is an artist of people. It is neuroscience. He is not consciously that canny. Allow me that much at least.

Version

'I have you to thank' he said,
easing himself from the couch,
'that, between the pair of us, we have reached a
definite conclusion:
I am the editor of *Aquarius* and you're the one
with identity confusion.'

The shrink shrank.
Then with true contrition
helped to crank up
this edition.

List of illustrations

Thank you, thank you, thank you!

In addition to the formal acknowledgements, we wish to thank equally sincerely: Mary Montague, our London Representative whose help in every aspect of the project was invaluable. Poets: Conor O' Callaghan and Vona Groarke (initial proofreading and formatting). Vona also helped with application forms. Lelia Doolan (for enthusiastic support and final proofreading). Ellen O'Hanlon (Accounts) Dundalgan Press (for scanning some of the artwork). Chris Hammond, Timothy Taylor Gallery, London (Craigie Aitchison artwork). Dean Kelly (for photographing some of the artwork and putting it on disc). Paul Johnson, Artists' Services Manager, The Irish Arts Council, who did his best. Dermot Ahern, for suggesting we apply to Cultures of Ireland among others. For their help in hosting the book launches: Sinead McCorry, Manager Waterstones Bookshop, Belfast, Jules Mann, Director, and Jessica York, The Poetry Society, London. Joseph Woods, Director, Poetry Ireland and Rosaleen Kearney, Director The Patrick Kavanagh Centre, Inniskeen.

We appreciated the courtesy, patience and professionalism of Tony O'Hanlon and Peggy McConnell of Propeller. Their skill and artistry is evident.

Finally, many personal thanks to Tony's family members Eoin and Toni-Louise, Colm, Kate and Donnacha for support and especially for IT advice; and to Rachel for patience and encouragement as a tide of manuscripts, discs, drafts and other documents engulfed room after room. Personal gratitude also to Constance's family, her daughter Deirdre and son Finn for their advice on IT and much more, her daughter Nessa for the lovely piece about their Christmases with Eddie and her beloved grandchild Ava for just being alive!

Míle Buíochas one and all.

New Island Publishers for *The Lives of the Poets* from Collected Poems by Anthony Cronin.

Department of English, NUI, Galway for *Baghdad* by Gabriel Rosenstock from ROPES Untwined.

London Review of Books, for *For Eddie Linden at Seventy* by Michael Longley.

Faber for *To My Mother* from Eros in Dogma (1944) by George Barker.

Jay Landesman Ltd. for *City of Razors,* and *Hampstead by Night* from *City of Razors* (1980) by Eddie Linden.

Carcanet Press (1988) for *Eddie and the Weevil* from Collected Poems by John Heath-Stubbs.

Polyantric Press for *Little Magazines* from A Bonus (1977) by Elizabeth Smart.

Salzburg University Press, for *Vocation* from The Wide World (An O'Grady Casebook) (2003) by Desmond O'Grady.

The Gallery Press and The Deerfield Press for *Thanks* by Robert Creeley.

The Gallery Press for the extract from *Cyrano de Bergerac* by Derek Mahon.

Chatto & Windus for *Knock-Knees, Bow-Legs* from The Knockabout Show by Gerda Mayer.

Les Ecrits des Forges/Le Temps des Cérises, (2003) for *La Cité de Rasoirs* Translated by Anne Talvaz. Published in Quarante et un poètes de la Grande-Bretagne.

Free Press for excerpt from *An Honourable Deception?* New Labour, Iraq, and the Misuse of Power (2003) by the Right Hon. Clare Short MP.

Cargo Press for *Odysseus speaking* under the title *No One speaking* from The Odysseus Poems: Fictions on The Odyssey of Homer (1999) by Judith Kazantzis.

City Tribune, Galway for *Edgware Road Station* by John Hogan in Writing in the West (1993)

The editors have made every effort to contact publishers of materials used in this book and apologise to those not acknowledged.